NAME THAT

BALLPLAYER

The Ultimate Baseball Quiz Book

Wayne Stewart

SKYHORSE PUBLISHING

Skyhorse Publishing books may be purchased in bulk at special discounts for sales promotion, corporate gifts, fund-raising, or educational purposes. Special editions can also be created to specifications. For details, contact the Special Sales Department, Skyhorse Publishing, 307 West 36th Street, 11th Floor, New York, NY 10018 or info@skyhorsepublishing.com.

Skyhorse® and Skyhorse Publishing® are registered trademarks of Skyhorse Publishing, Inc.®, a Delaware corporation.

Visit our website at www.skyhorsepublishing.com.

10 9 8 7 6 5 4 3 2 1

Library of Congress Cataloging-in-Publication Data is available on file.

Cover design by Daniel Brount
Cover photo credit Getty Images

ISBN: 978-1-5107-4908-5
Ebook ISBN 978-1-62636-893-4

Printed in the United States of America

For the latest addition to the Stewart lineup, my grandson Nathan Stewart.

CONTENTS

INTRODUCTION AND
HOW TO PLAY

Quite some time ago, there was a television game show called *Name That Tune*. Contestants on the show would predict how many musical notes it would take them to recognize a song. The player who placed the lowest "bid" was given the chance to listen to a few notes, and then it was time to name that tune. This book is set up along a similar premise.

If you can name that ballplayer on the first clue, you will be awarded five points. If you require a second clue, take three points, and if you need a third clue, you can still salvage one point. Using this system, you can compare your grand total with that of another player who also owns this book.

However, if you *really* want to keep the baseball motif going, there's another way to keep score: Nail the identity of the player in question on the first clue and give yourself a home run; on the second clue, credit yourself with a double; and score a single if you identify the player on the third and final clue.

So, throughout the book, think of yourself as a batter with each clue representing a pitch—three strikes and you're out. You'll have to take a hike back to the bench before moving on to your next at bat.

Keep in mind players' statistics and feats mentioned are through the end of the 2019 regular season, and, therefore, do not include any awards bestowed for that year.

Each chapter represents a portion of our imaginary game. Beginning with "Batting Practice," in which you will be tossed some easy lobs, try to rack up sure points because each chapter gets increasingly more difficult. In the next chapter, "The Early Innings," things start off relatively slowly and in an exploratory manner, much like the first three innings of a typical baseball game. In "The Middle Innings," things start to get more serious, with the questions increasing in difficulty. Sometimes the players in question won't be as famous as those in earlier chapters, and sometimes the problem is more difficult, since the clues may be a bit vague on purpose. "The Stretch Innings" may be a true challenge to many readers, as you will be presented with somewhat obscure players and/or be given less obvious clues; here, you may find out if you're a good two-strike hitter. A brief final chapter, "Extra Innings," is a sort of "Down to the Last Strike" situation which follows with its own special rules: You get one quick question with limited clues, and you either come up big in the clutch or fail. Then there's the Bonus section, which covers active players in 2019. So, stretch your brain and memory, and step up to the plate—enjoy!

☉ ☉ ☉ **1** ☉ ☉ ☉

BATTING PRACTICE

Just as players routinely take batting practice—they shorten the term to "BP"—to loosen up and work on their game, in this chapter you will be presented with some easy offerings, soft tosses, as it were, for you to jack out of the park. Build up your points early, because in the late innings of the book, things will become a bit nasty—again, it's just like a real baseball game. Some pitches early in the game don't seem to have quite the importance of those deep into the game. Then the blazing fast and filthy breaking stuff comes at you late in the game off a starter who has lasting power, like a Bob Gibson or a closer such as a Mariano Rivera.

1 A. This Hall of Fame flamethrower of a pitcher was traded along with three other players from the Mets to the Angels in December of 1971, when he was just 24 years old, for Jim Fregosi (who would wind up with a .265 lifetime batting average) in one of the most lopsided trades ever engineered.

B. The first player to earn $1 million in a season, he packed fans into ballparks across the nation with his 100+ mph fastball; fans knew that the possibilities of a no-hitter occurring and/or a strikeout record tumbling were palpable every time he took to the hill.

C. This ageless wonder broke Sandy Koufax's single-season record when he whiffed 383 batters in 1973, one of 11 times he led his league in Ks. In fact, he was still fanning 200 to 300 hitters when he was as old as 44. His best total as an "old-timer" came in 1989 when, at the age of 42, he struck out 301 men. Bottom-line numbers: an ungodly 27 seasons pitched, 324 wins, a best-ever total of 5,714 strikeouts, and a lifetime ERA of 3.19.

2 A. During the off-season after the 2006 World Series, this man inked a $126 million contract (leaving the A's for the Giants) that would cover seven years and make him the highest-paid pitcher at the time, earning about a half-million dollars each time he took to the hill.

B. A three-time All-Star, this southpaw won 23 games in 2002, which propelled him to capture the Cy Young Award that year. However, by 2008 things had soured, and he posted a 10–17 record with a bloated ERA of 5.15.

C. He is one of only a smattering of men with the last initial of "Z" to make it to the majors.

3 A. This Yankees center fielder hit .325 lifetime and was married to one of Hollywood's most glamorous stars.

B. His brothers, both big leaguers, were Vince and Dom. The man in question had more homers than strikeouts in a record seven seasons.

C. He was known as the "Yankee Clipper" and he was baseball's first $100,000-per-season player (1949).

4 A. This smooth center fielder, who spent nearly his entire career with the Giants, robbed so many batters on deep drives to the outfield that a writer once gushed that this player's glove was where "triples go to die." His catches were often as spectacular as a Hawaiian sunset.

B. Until his godson Barry Bonds came along, only Hank Aaron and Babe Ruth had hit more than his 660 homers, but this Hall of Famer was much more than just a power hitter—he could do it all, and was a true "five-tool" ballplayer. Surprisingly, even though he chased home 1,902 runs, he never led his league in RBIs.

Seemingly only a pact with Lucifer could produce a more complete package of a player.

C. His colorful nickname was "The Say Hey Kid."

5 A. His real name is listed as Denton True _____, but because he threw like a cyclone, he earned a different name. Any way you look at it, though, he's the ultimate name in pitching. He owns fifteen 20-win seasons, and his 511 lifetime victories is one record experts believe will endure forever.

B. He won nearly 62 percent of all his decisions, racked up three no-hitters (one of them was a perfect game), and lived from just after the Civil War until several years after the Korean War. He is the only man to throw a no-hitter in both the nineteenth and twentieth centuries.

C. If you haven't got this one by now, try this clue: The premier yearly award given to the game's top pitcher is named after this man.

6 A. Hardly a superstar, this former St. Louis Cardinal is as pesky and as tiny—listed at 5-foot-7 and 165 pounds—as a splinter.

B. He came to the Cardinals via the Angels, where he was a member of the 2002 world champions.

C. When his Cards won it all in 2006, he once again proved his worth, winning the MVP of the World Series. He spent 2008 with Toronto and Arizona, then finished his career as a Padre.

7 A. When the first-ever election was held for the Baseball Hall of Fame, this man received more votes than any other baseball legend, and thus became one of five charter members in the Hall.

B. Known for his volatility, he was equally famous for his passionate drive. When he was young, before he became a major leaguer, his mother had shot and killed his father, and a theory holds that this man was, in effect, obsessively still trying to show his father just how good he was.

C. One of his quotes says it all about this fiery outfielder who was known as "The Georgia Peach": "I had to be first all the time—first in everything. All I ever thought about was winning."

8 A. There's a misconception that this all-time great was born in Commerce, Oklahoma, given his nickname, "The Commerce Comet." His actual birthplace was Spavinaw, Oklahoma.

  B. He followed Joe DiMaggio among a string of stellar outfielders—specifically center fielders, in their cases—for the Yankees.

  C. His power is unquestioned, and he was the ultimate switch-hitting slugger.

9 A. In 2006, this man became the first catcher to win the American League (AL) batting title when he hit .347. In fact, that average made him the first catcher ever who led the entire majors in hitting. In 2008 and 2009 he nailed down two more batting crowns, with batting averages of .328 and .365.

  B. His first taste of big league play came in 2004 when he played 35 games for the Twins as a 21 year old.

  C. The St. Paul, Minnesota, native made the 2006 All-Star team, his first of six, and finished in the top ten for the MVP Award as well.

10 A. He's played for the Phillies, where he won the Rookie of the Year Award in 1997, and the Cardinals, where he appeared frequently in postseason play. He owns a 2006 World Series ring but made bigger headlines for his feud with St. Louis manager Tony LaRussa. Their disputes eventually led to his being traded to Toronto for Troy Glaus in 2008. He finished his career wearing a Reds uniform.

  B. He owns Gold Gloves galore, eight in all, for his toil at the hot corner.

  C. His most outstanding season was 2004, when he established single-season highs of 34 HR, 124 RBIs, and a .314 batting average. That season he finished fourth in MVP voting.

11 A. In 2004, this righty won 18 games and the *Sporting News* selected him as their Pitcher of the Year.

  B. The previous season he led the National League (NL) in ERA with a sparkling 2.34. In 2002, 2003, 2004, and 2006 he was among the league leaders for strikeouts, with his third-place finish in 2004 (with 151 whiffs) being his personal best.

C. He broke in with the Atlanta Braves, then moved on to the Pirates before becoming a Giant, but was with the Dodgers to end his playing days in 2009.

12 A. This Hall of Fame outfielder hit an amazing .345 lifetime (from 1907 to 1928). His nickname was "The Gray Eagle." He was the first man to win the World Series in his first full season as a manager—in 1920 with the Indians.

B. He shares the same initials with fellow Hall of Famer who went by the nickname "Tom Terrific."

C. In the Dead Ball Era (1900–19), this man played such a shallow center field that he became, in effect, a fifth infielder. As a matter of fact, at times he positioned himself so near to second base, he set a record when he was responsible for turning six unassisted double plays. It wasn't that uncommon for him to come in on, say, a sinking line drive, snag it, then dash to second base to retire a runner who had drifted too far from that bag. He even, on occasion, took part in sneak-in pickoff plays, taking the throw from a swiveling pitcher to gun down a stunned runner at second.

13 A. The success this Hall of Famer had with his wicked splitter, which he relied upon heavily, changed the game of baseball. He once stated that without that pitch, he would have been, at the very best, a "Double-A player."

B. When he retired in 1988, his 300 saves stood third place on the all-time list, trailing only two other greats of the game, Rollie Fingers and Goose Gossage.

C. In a 2006 ceremony, the St. Louis Cardinals retired his number 42 jersey, which had already been retired by the Cards and every other big league club to honor Jackie Robinson. This pitcher also worked for the Cubs and the Braves.

14 A. When the pitcher from the above question won his Cy Young in 1979, this man came in second, and his Houston Astros

teammate, J. R. Richard, came in third. Both the man in question and his older brother were knuckleball specialists; his brother won more than 300 games and was voted into the Hall of Fame.

B. One of the most infamous moments in this player's career came when he was caught with a nail file in his uniform pocket, allegedly in his possession, of course, to doctor the baseball. Shortly after, during his suspension for that rules violation, he made an appearance on a television talk show, coming on stage wearing a carpenter's apron and lugging a power sander.

C. This man's son, Lance, also made it to the big league level, albeit not as a pitcher.

15 A. This outfielder was an instrumental part of the Indians' success in the 1990s and went on to help the Red Sox win a World Series.

B. Many considered him to be as lacking on defense as he was awesome on offense. He was labeled a sort of scatterbrain and was even said to have suffered from Attention Deficit Disorder. However, he let his bat speak for him: He was a .312 lifetime hitter who accumulated 555 homers. Further, in 1999, his incredible 165 RBIs was the best output since Jimmie Foxx back in 1938. By 2008 he had worn out his welcome in Boston and was sent to the Dodgers in a three-way swap which brought Jason Bay to the Red Sox.

C. During a game in 2005, the Red Sox pitching coach visited pitcher Wade Miller and the player in question entered Fenway Park's Green Monster, vanishing from the playing field. When Miller was ready to resume pitching, the outfielder had still not taken his position in left field. Experts could not recall another time that such a bizarre moment had occurred on a big league diamond.

16 A. This Hall of Famer is a native of Panama, born on a train in 1945 in the town of Gatun.

B. He hit line drives as straight and as low to the ground as Florida's "Alligator Alley." In 1977, the year he was the American League's MVP, he won one of his seven batting crowns, ripping the ball to a .388 tune, then the highest average since Ted Williams hit .406 in 1941.

C. He spent his entire career with the Twins and the Angels, playing second base, and then, in the second half of his career, first base.

17 A. This all-time great hailed from Donora, Pennsylvania, born there on November 21, 1920. He finished his illustrious 22-year career with 3,630 hits. Oddly, exactly half of those hits came at home and half during road trips.

B. He won the NL MVP in 1943, 1946, and 1948. Hank Aaron, Willie Mays, and this man are the only greats ever to have played in 24 All-Star games.

C. He won the batting crown a sensational seven times, had a colorful nickname, and was one of the game's most amiable and respected men. A statue of him stands outside the park in the city where he played for his entire career.

18 A. This outfielder, a fellow Hall of Famer, not only comes from the same hometown as the man in the question above, but he was also born on the same date. Additionally, his father, a lifetime .296 hitter, is also a Donora, Pennsylvania, native.

B. He was so talented that he broke in at a very young age, 19 in 1989, making him the second-youngest player in the majors that season. That fact spawned his nickname, "The Kid," although he also goes by "Junior."

C. From his early days with the Mariners, where he became the first player to appear in a big league game with his father, to his stint with the Reds, then to the White Sox and back to Seattle, this man did it all, pounding out 630 homers.

19 A. Until Hank Aaron and Eddie Mathews combined forces to swat their 773rd career home run *as teammates* in 1965, Ruth and this man held the record.

B. On May 31, 1925, this man began the most fantastic durability streak in sports history, one that lasted until Cal Ripken Jr. finally blew by this venerable achievement.

C. He had 100 or more runs and runs driven in during each of his 13 full seasons, once hit four homers in a single contest, and, power aside (and he *did* crank out 493 homers), he hit a lofty .340 lifetime. Incidentally, this man was the first ever to have his uniform number retired.

20 A. This hard-hitting first baseman/designated hitter enjoyed a revival year in 2006, helping the A's to a playoff bid and a sweep over the Twins in the American League Division Series (ALDS), where he hit a cool .500.

B. His previous 16 years were all spent with the White Sox, where he won the MVP in both 1993 and 1994. He spent 2007 and part of 2008 with Toronto before returning to the A's.

C. His nickname, "The Big Hurt," was quite fitting, as he really put a sting on the ball, inflicting pain on opposing pitchers. Over 19 seasons he crushed 521 homers.

21 A. This man has been famous since his fabulous days on high school diamonds, starring at Westminster Christian School in Miami. There, he hit .477 with 42 steals in 35 games, but his big power surge was still a few years away—he finished his career with 696 (somewhat tainted) homers.

B. His breakout season came in 1996 in his first full big league season. All he did was lead the American League in hitting (.358), doubles, runs, and RBIs. He also belted 36 homers and established new records by a shortstop for runs, hits, doubles, extra base hits, and slugging percentage. A move to third base would come later.

C. When this player's name is mentioned, most people probably think about his enormous salary, but after his disappearing act in the 2006 postseason (one single in 14 at-bats) and again in 2007 (4-for-15 with but one RBI), some critics instead pointed to his difficulties with hitting in vital spots instead.

22 A. As is still the case with "Shoeless" Joe Jackson, the debate still rages over whether or not this all-time luminary—from 1963, when he was the NL Rookie of the Year, through 1986—belongs in the Hall of Fame.

B. This man always hustled on the field and had a burning, Ty Cobb–like desire to win. He played every infield position except short, and all three outfield spots, though rarely center field, over his career. While his last name is the same as that of a flower, there has been a figurative stench, and a red—as in Cincinnati Reds and as in scarlet—letter associated with him due to his gambling, a baseball taboo.

C. If those clues aren't enough, "all-time hit king" should wrap it up.

23 A. For years this steady, highly productive ballplayer put up big numbers but didn't get much ink. Things soon changed after he emphatically testified before a congressional committee that he did not do steroids. Not long after his denial he started getting a lot of the wrong kind of publicity when it was discovered that he *had*, in fact, taken steroids.

B. His lifetime statistics are Hall of Fame–worthy (3,020 hits, #29 all-time; 585 doubles, #20; 1,835 RBIs, #17; and 569 HR, #13), but speculation is that the temperature in Hades would have to dip into the lower 30s before he'd be voted into Cooperstown.

C. The only time he was ever traded was from the Cubs, along with Jamie Moyer and Drew Hall, for reliever Mitch Williams and five other Rangers back in December of 1988.

24 A. This Hall of Famer ranks first for the most lifetime homers launched by a switch-hitter in NL play—468. He also won his only batting crown in 2008 when he hit a lofty .364, by far his highest average, as a 36-year-old. The next season that average plummeted by exactly 100 points.

B. Mainly a third baseman, he played some outfield for the Braves, the only team he played for since he broke in back in 1993. By 1999, he took home MVP honors when he led

Atlanta (who would win the pennant but get swept by the Yankees) to the playoffs while hitting a personal high of 45 home runs.

C. His real first name is Larry but he goes by a much peppier nickname. Meanwhile, his last name is one of the most common surnames in the United States.

25 A. This Hall of Famer's nickname gives his first name away, "King Carl," but he was also known as the "Meal Ticket."

B. And what a meal ticket he was, winning 253 games, good for a marvelous .622 winning percentage from 1928 through 1943 for the New York Giants. From 1936 to 1937, he posted a record 24 consecutive wins.

C. He remains the most famous practitioner of a painful pitch, the screwball. He utilized that pitch quite effectively when he set down five big-name AL luminaries in the 1934 All-Star Game: Babe Ruth, Lou Gehrig, Jimmie Foxx, Al Simmons, and Joe Cronin.

26 A. Already a recognized superstar by 2006, when he was just 23 years old, this third baseman/designated hitter/outfielder played that season under a contract that rewarded him with only $472,000. By winning his 2007 arbitration case, he earned $7.4 million the following season. His 2019 paycheck was for $30 million.

B. In 2006 he trailed only one NL hitter in his quest for a batting crown, annihilating the ball to a .339 tune. In his first three full seasons he's swatted 33, 33, and 26 round-trippers, but that merely foreshadowed his two seasons of 44 homers. In fact, among active players back in 2006, only Ken Griffey Jr., Alex Rodriguez, Andruw Jones, and Albert Pujols had hit more homers than this man before reaching the age of 24. Griffey led the way with 132, while this player had 108.

C. The native of Venezuela, who won a Triple Crown, has played for the Florida Marlins and the Detroit Tigers. In 2003, his very first year in the majors, his Marlins won it all, but, stunningly, despite another fine season in 2008 by this star, neither he nor the other studs he was surrounded by could hoist the highly touted (in the preseason) Tigers out of the cellar.

27 A. What a year this lefty put together in 1978. On June 17, he whiffed 18 batters and logged a stupendous 25–3 record, winning almost 90 percent of his decisions (.889, highest ever in a season by a 20-game winner). His tiny ERA of 1.74, his nine shutouts, and his 248 Ks allowed him to waltz his way to the Cy Young Award, winning it unanimously.

B. Due to his Lafayette, Louisiana, roots, he was nicknamed "Gator" and "Louisiana Lightning."

C. He was a coach under Joe Torre with the Yankees, the only team he pitched for.

28 A. On April 20 of America's bicentennial year, this young man made his debut. It took a slew of adjectives to describe this colorful pitcher: gawky, refreshing, childlike, eccentric. While he was on the mound he talked to the baseball, often instructing it where to go.

B. His physical appearance soon gave birth to a nickname based on a popular *Sesame Street* character.

C. He became a national sensation overnight, packing not only Tiger Stadium, but every park in which he appeared. He won the Rookie of the Year Award, going 19–9, started the All-Star Game as a rookie, and led the league with his infinitesimal 2.34 ERA.

29 A. He was a monster of a man back in the 1930s. In fact, one of his nicknames was "The Beast." He may have been strong (534 lifetime home runs), but by today's standards he was, at 6 feet tall and 195 pounds, hardly imposing.

B. He won back-to-back MVPs in 1932 and 1933, the season he won the Triple Crown, and took home another MVP plaque in 1938. He inflicted a wasp-like sting with his bat, once hitting 58 homers and once driving home 175 runs. On one occasion he drew a record six walks in a nine-inning game.

C. His other nickname, "Double X," ties in with the unusual way his last name was spelled and should, therefore, give this man's identity away.

30 A. With all due respect to Willie Mays, some say this player, who retired after the 2012 season, is the greatest, smoothest defensive center fielder of all time. His 10 Gold Gloves (only Mays and Roberto Clemente with 12 have more) lends credence to that. Furthermore, he excelled there since a very young age; his first full season was in 1997 when he was just 20 years old, and he won his Gold Glove Awards every season from 1998 through 2007.

B. He is one of just two men to drill home runs in his first two World Series at bats, doing so in 1996 versus the Yankees. His first homer made him, at 19, the youngest player ever to connect in World Series play, topping the old record established by Mickey Mantle.

C. While he had always been considered, at the least, a very solid hitter, he exploded in 2005 with 51 home runs. However, inexplicably, he folded in 2007 with the Braves (hitting just .222) and in 2008 with the Dodgers (.158, three homers, and a mere 14 ribbies).

31 A. In 1940, because of the pitching heroics of this Cleveland Indians star, every member of the Chicago White Sox exited a ball game with exactly the same batting average they had at game's start. The trick here is that, since the game was the season's opener, each man came in sporting an average of .000, and due to the fact that this man threw a no-hitter, everyone stayed stuck on .000.

B. In 1936 he pitched his first big league game ever straight off an Iowa farm, while still a student in high school. He would soon go on to become the first pitcher to win 20 before he had reached the age of 21. As a matter of fact, until Dwight Gooden came along, this man remained the youngest pitcher to hit the 20-win plateau when he went 24–9 in 1939.

C. He set the record for lifetime one-hitters with 12, won 266 games, and, armed with his "heater," this native of Van Meter also led the AL in Ks on seven occasions.

32 A. During his playing career (1897–1917), the man known as "The Flying Dutchman" never earned even close to what his 1909 baseball card was worth. In 2016, for example, the card was sold for a record $3.1 million.

B. This man is still considered by many to be the greatest shortstop of all time, with his .328 lifetime batting average, 3,420 hits, and eight batting titles.

C. He is one of the five original members of the Hall of Fame, and a statue of this player has stood outside Forbes Field, Three Rivers Stadium, and now PNC Park.

33 A. When the Montreal Expos had Warren Cromartie and Andre Dawson patrolling two of the outfield spots in 1982 and 1983, this Hall of Fame speed burner was in left field.

B. Nicknamed "Rock," he and Rickey Henderson were that era's kings of the base paths, and this man wound up with 808 stolen bases.

C. His .847 lifetime success rate in stealing is the best ever among men with 400 or more attempts. On the downside, following the 1982 season he underwent rehab for a cocaine problem.

34 A. The Expos of this player's era had several talented outfielders, such as Ellis Valentine and, for one season (1980), this man, with the initials "R.L." He would go on to become the first player to top both leagues in stolen bases.

B. A native of Detroit, this player was originally signed by the Detroit Tigers in 1974, although the big story was not so much the signing but his background. As a youngster he was a dropout, was arrested for the first time at the age of 15, shot heroin, and served time in prison for armed robbery, having been sentenced for 5 to 15 years in a state prison in Michigan.

C. Tigers manager Billy Martin saw this man when he was in prison, arranged for him to get a day parole and a tryout, and ultimately managed him as a big leaguer. This player went on to lead his league in steals twice.

35 A. In 2006 this Texas outfielder, nicknamed "Little Sarge" (his father, who played big league ball for 16 seasons, was called, of course, "Sarge") experienced a boon year, stroking the ball for personal highs in virtually every offensive category while becoming an All-Star for the first and only time.

B. A great leaper, his July 1, 2006, catch robbed Mike Lamb of a sure home run, leading a longtime observer to call the catch the best defensive play made by a Texas Ranger over a period of 26 years.

C. He bounced around the bigs, playing for a total of seven clubs from 1999 to 2010, including the Padres and the Mets twice.

36 A. This man, who began his career with the Royals, also played a good chunk, four years, of his career with the Red Sox. He was a very popular figure in Boston until he defected to the rival Yankees in 2006 as a free agent. After that, Bostonians took to giving him nicknames such as "Judas."

B. As part of the Red Sox "bunch of idiots," he gained fame not only for his playing, but also for his beard and long flowing locks.

C. In 2006 this fine center fielder joined Stan Musial and Lou Gehrig as the only players ever to swat 30+ doubles and score 100 or more runs for nine years running. He owned 2,769 lifetime hits over his 18-year career, which ended in 2012.

37 A. A powerful slugger, this 6-foot-6, 275-pound Cincinnati Reds outfielder spanked 46 HR in 2004, then crushed exactly 40 homers each season from 2005 through 2008.

B. In 2004 he drove home 100+ runs for the first time, but struck out 195 times to break the former single-season record held by Bobby Bonds (since broken several times). In 2012 he turned a rather unusual trick, leading his league in walks and in strikeouts with a new personal high of an ungodly 222 K's. Through 2019, only Mark Reynolds exceeded his single season total, setting the new record by one whiff. Only two men, Reggie

14

Jackson and Jim Thome, have ever gone down on strikes more than his 2,379 strikeouts.

C. After throwing for almost 5,000 yards as a quarterback in high school, he attended college at the University of Texas where he was the backup quarterback to Major Applewhite for one season. When the Longhorns then committed to QB Chris Simms, son of former NFL quarterback Phil, the man in question was asked to switch his position to tight end; he opted to pursue a baseball career instead.

38 A. A member of the "Boys of Summer" Brooklyn Dodgers, this man won three MVPs.

B. He made the Hall of Fame despite having his career curtailed when he was paralyzed in a January 1958 automobile accident. Somehow he stayed buoyant throughout all of his tribulations, entitling his autobiography *It's Good to be Alive*.

C. In 1953 he hit 40 homers while working behind the plate, a record high for catchers until Todd Hundley eclipsed that total by one in 1996.

39 A. Known for his unusual batting style, this player finished his 22-year major league stint with 509 homers.

B. A Tampa, Florida, native, he went to the same high school as his uncle, Dwight Gooden. He is also the cousin of NFL wide receiver Tim Carter. Further, in the 1980 Little League World Series, this slugger and another future big leaguer, Derek Bell, were on the same Tampa Bay squad.

C. He spent 2004 through 2006 with the Yankees; in April 2005 he got into a scuffle with a Boston fan who took a swing at the volatile outfielder as he was preparing to field a ball.

40 A. This pitcher, famous for throwing a specialty pitch, made a vow to himself that he'd nail down his 300th career victory without using said pitch as a way to prove he was more than a one-trick pony. Then, with two outs in the ninth, he reconsidered, feeling it was only appropriate to utilize his out pitch to wrap things up.

B. That pitch was taught to both him and his brother, Joe (who won 221 contests, making this the winningest brother act ever in the majors), by their father.

C. A Hall of Famer, this man enjoyed many of his finest years as a baseball graybeard.

41 A. One of the most colorful players ever, he was equally famous for butchering the English language. Consider his famous quote from his days as an announcer: "Don't fail to miss tomorrow's game."

B. Another time, after his brother Daffy had pitched a no-hitter in the nightcap of a doubleheader, this man, who had tossed a three-hitter in the opening game, stated, "If I knew you was going to pitch a no-hitter, I would have pitched one too."

C. He is the last man to win 30 games in the National League. His career was cut short due to injury, but he packed the vast majority of his 150 wins over a five-year stretch.

42 A. This pitcher, one of a handful of men with 300 wins and 3,000 strikeouts, has been compared to the Sears line of tools in that he is a true craftsman, making his living on the edges of home plate. In the 1990s no man won more than this control artist.

B. Most of his glory years were spent with the Atlanta Braves, where he won three of his four successive Cy Young Awards as part of an illustrious pitching staff that also featured John Smoltz and Tom Glavine, fellow Cy Young winners.

C. In 1995, he sizzled with a 19–2 slate and a minuscule ERA of 1.63 when the league average was 4.23. Of course, the year before his ERA stood proudly at 1.56. For his entire 23-year career, he walked fewer than two men per nine innings pitched—in 1997, he issued only 20 bases on balls over 232 $\frac{2}{3}$ frames.

43 A. Originally a pitcher for Houston, he stood fourth on the list of active players with the lowest lifetime ERA as late as 2008. (3.13)

B. He won in double digits each of his first eight seasons with the Astros, reaching 20 wins in 2004 and 2005, and his career won-loss percentage was then an astronomical .668. He ended his career at .615.

C. On June 11, 2003, he was the starter when Houston no-hit the Yankees and set a record for a "no-no" by using six pitchers to complete the performance.

44 A. He was a player (586 lifetime homers, tenth best ever, more than 1,800 RBIs, and nearly 3,000 hits), a player-manager (when he became baseball's first African American manager with Cleveland), and worked again as a manager after his playing days were over (with the Giants, Orioles, and, most recently, with the Expos/Nationals). In short, he's a Hall of Famer.

B. He broke in with the Reds and won the 1961 MVP just a handful of years into his career. Then, prior to the 1966 season, when the Cincinnati brass felt he was getting too old to keep—club owner Bill DeWitt labeled this man "an old 30"—he was swapped to Baltimore where he promptly won the Triple Crown and the MVP, becoming the first (and thus far, only) man to win that award in both leagues.

C. His accomplishments were foreshadowed in 1956 when he won the Rookie of the Year Award and made the All-Star team during his inaugural season.

45 A. As was the case with the man from the previous question, this shortstop took just a few years before he copped an MVP Award (in 2002). At the time he was with the Oakland A's in his fifth full season in the majors.

B. About seven weeks after he was granted free-agency status in October of 2003, he made like a carpetbagger, fled Oakland, and signed with the Orioles. In 2004 he rewarded Baltimore fans by contributing a terrific 150 RBIs and 34 HR, both career highs.

C. Highly vivacious and demonstrative, he was durable (he once put together a long string of consecutive games played—1,152 contests—not unlike another famous O's shortstop). He hit a personal high of .330 in 2006 and was an All-Star six times, winning the All-Star Game's MVP trophy in 2005.

46 A. In spring training of 2007 it was disclosed that this man, a 6-foot-3 pitcher who was *listed* at 250 pounds, was wearing a size 58 jersey, said to be the largest size ever for a big leaguer—no wonder they call him "Boomer."

B. He has a fascination with Babe Ruth and once purchased a Yankees baseball cap worn by Ruth in 1936 for a reported $35,000. He wore the hat in a game until an umpire made him remove it. Also to honor Ruth, this man wore #3 for part of the 2005 season with Boston. When he was with the Yankees, who had, of course, retired that number, he wore double threes (#33) instead of #3. He stated that wearing #33 allowed him to "be Babe Ruth twice over."

C. He was born in Torrance, California, and attended the same high school, San Diego's Point Loma High, as Don Larsen, and, like Larsen, this man threw a perfect game while wearing the Yankees uniform.

47 A. When this Yankee, whose first name is the same as the man from the previous question, threw *his* perfect game in 1999, Larsen just happened to be in attendance, taking part in "Yogi Berra Day" at Yankee Stadium by throwing out the ceremonial first pitch.

B. He was a big strikeout artist (his personal high was 261 Ks in 1992) who won the Cy Young Award when he was with the Royals in 1994.

C. The ten-year gap between his two 20-win seasons is reportedly the longest ever for a big league pitcher. His fans came to be known as "Coneheads."

48 A. This charter member of the Hall of Fame spent his youth in St. Mary's Industrial School.

B. He began his career as a left-handed pitcher who once led the league with a microscopic ERA of 1.75.

C. Later, as an outfielder, he earned the nickname "The Sultan of Swat." Clearly he was, to his contemporaries, what Gulliver was to the Lilliputians.

49 A. He's often called "the greatest hitter who ever lived," and he displayed his prowess year in and year out. Only once in his career did he hit below .316, and that was in 1959 when he was 40 years old and injured for much of the year. He even hit a whopping .388 in 1957, ending that season at the age of 39. Lifetime he was a wonderful .344 hitter—and don't forget his 500+ doubles and homers and his 1,839 RBIs.

B. He accomplished all of that despite missing four and a half seasons to serve in both World War II and the Korean War; experts marvel at what numbers he would have put up given an extra four and a half years. As a side note, he flew 38 missions in Korea, walked away from a fiery crash landing of his fighter jet, and flew with a then-unknown John Glenn.

C. Of course, many fans think of one thing when they hear his name—he was the last man to hit .400, and did so by refusing to skip playing in a season-ending doubleheader to sit on and preserve his .400 average (he entered that day with a batting average of .39955, officially .400). For the record, he came up big in that twin bill, winding up with a .406 mark in 1941, his third season in the majors.

50 A. He's a powerful first baseman, although he broke in as a catcher. He spent 2006 through 2009 with the Mets, and 2005 with Florida, but first established himself as a star with the Blue Jays. Projected over a full 162 games played, he could be expected to pop about 40 homers yearly and drive in around 120. He wound up with 473 career home runs.

B. In the 2006 National League Division Series (NLDS), he was highly instrumental in putting the Dodgers away, homering in the opening contest and hitting .429 over the three-game sweep. That same season he became just the fourth player to swat 30+ home runs in ten consecutive seasons. He once drilled four homers in a single game, doing so on September 25, 2003.

C. In 2004 he became involved in controversy when he refused to be a part of the playing of "God Bless America" during his games' seventh-inning stretches; instead, he chose to stay in his dugout as a protest against the war in Iraq.

51 A. Prior to the man mentioned above, this outfielder was the last AL player to come up big with a four-home-run game. His splash of fame came on May 2, 2002, when he was with Seattle as their center fielder.

B. In 2000 this three-time Gold Glover with the initials "M.C." was involved in the multi-player deal that sent him from the Reds to the M's, with Ken Griffey Jr. going to Cincy. He spent 2008 with Milwaukee, hitting 25 HR. His last two productive seasons were with Milwaukee, where he slugged 25 then 24 HR.

C. In 2005 he and Carlos Beltran crashed together in one of base-ball's ugliest, most bone-jarring collisions when they both dove for the ball. The man in question was toted off the field on a stretcher, having suffered multiple fractures to his nose and cheekbones.

52 A. A member of the Hall of Fame, Class of 2005, this popular Cubs infielder retired from the game partway through the 1994 sea-son, upset with his performance and too proud to take what he felt would be an undeserved paycheck. He couldn't stay away from the game he loved too long, though, and was back in 1996.

B. In his first big league season, 1981, he played just 13 games for the Phillies. Traded the following season to Chicago, along with Larry Bowa for Ivan DeJesus, he would spend 15 years with the Cubs. His most memorable day of that tenure may well have been his two-homer performance on national television in June of 1984, with both smashes coming off the nearly untouchable Bruce Sutter.

C. A real gimme clue: He was named after former big league pitcher Ryne Duren.

53 A. He was a vital part of the Reds' "Big Red Machine" and spent his entire career in Cincinnati. He is considered an all-time elite at his position, and in 1989 gained even more glory in Cooperstown, a far cry from his home in Binger, Oklahoma, where he was the class valedictorian.

B. He's won every award imaginable—Rookie of the Year in 1968, MVP in 1970 and 1972, World Series MVP in 1976, Gold Gloves galore, the 1975 Lou Gehrig Award, ad infinitum. Plus, he's given credit for changing the way his position was played; he used a hinged mitt and began using a one-handed style of catching the ball.

C. He can hold seven baseballs in one hand, not a bad ability for a catcher. Finally, he was selected as the catcher on the Major League Baseball All-Time Team.

54 A. He is one of four AL pitchers to chalk up 16 straight wins in a single season (1912), just three shy of the all-time record held by Rube Marquard.

B. Over his career (1907–27), this Washington Senators fastball artist set myriad records, including the most lifetime shutouts, 110. Sadly, his team was full of futility and he made it to only two World Series, where he went 2–2 despite a sterling 2.16 ERA.

C. He led his league in wins six times, in ERA five times (with a hard-to-believe low of 1.14 in 1913), and remained the all-time King of Ks until Nolan Ryan usurped that title many decades later.

55 A. This man also won 16 in a row during AL play; he did this with the Yankees in 2001.

B. He has also won a mind-boggling seven Cy Young Awards, more than any man, ever.

C. His fastball is rocket-like, and with 354 wins and 4,672 strike-outs, he is clearly one of the greatest pitchers ever (although his stats, like others from the Steroid Era, came under scrutiny).

56 A. When the Pirates beat the Yankees in the bottom of the ninth inning in Game 7 of the 1960 World Series, this man, normally a catcher, was in left field and was resigned to watch the ball sail over his head.

B. A Hall of Famer, he was known as a bad ball hitter who rarely whiffed; in five seasons he had more homers than strikeouts. Born Lawrence Peter _____, he is known by a nickname that sounds like that of a cartoon character.

C. Although he amusingly butchered the language, he was no joke—he won three MVP Awards, all in the 1950s.

57 A. Although he'll (probably) never be in the Hall of Fame, he is one of just two men to hit .400 in a season and *not* win a batting title. In 1911, he hit .408, only to lose the crown to Ty Cobb and his .420 average.

B. Much has been made of the fact that this man was illiterate, and some say his lack of education and his naiveté were factors in his decision to accept money from gamblers who fixed the 1919 World Series.

C. The most colorful facet of this man was probably his nickname, "Shoeless Joe."

58 A. In 2001, the World Series was dominated by two pitchers, so it was only fitting that this man, playing for Arizona, shared the Series MVP with Randy Johnson.

B. Media friendly as a player, he's been known to make phone calls to sports talk shows, and he communicates with fans via the Internet. His credentials glisten: He was a three-time runner-up in Cy Young voting, had a .597 won-loss percentage, and more than 3,000 strikeouts. His best years were with the Phillies, Diamondbacks, and Red Sox.

C. In postseason play this Alaska-born righty was nearly invincible (10–2, 2.23 ERA). He'll forever be remembered for his one red (bloody) sock when he helped the Red Sox storm back from a 3–0 deficit to win the 2004 American League Championship Series (ALCS) and then win the World Series.

59 A. In 1968, pitchers from the Cardinals and Giants fired no-hitters on successive days. One was Ray Washburn; this man was the other, a future Hall of Famer who went on to become a 300-game winner, notching his historic win with Seattle where he was called "The Ancient Mariner."

B. Both he and his brother Jim own Cy Young Awards, a baseball first. In fact, this man is rare in that he owns a Cy Young Award in both leagues. Only the Niekro brothers own more wins than this brother combo. Also, these brothers were the first to pitch in the same All-Star Game (1970).

C. He would joke and deny that he applied foreign substances to the ball, but the title of his autobiography was *Me and the Spitter*.

60 A. Over the years when this Hall of Fame reliever entered a home game in San Diego, it was lights out and music level up—the song *Hell's Bells* roared over the PA system to greet him. Although aging by baseball standards, he was still going strong in his late thirties and into his forties, piling up 155 saves from 2006 through 2009. In 2006, at 38, he became the oldest pitcher to lead his league in saves with 46. Furthermore, that total represented his second-best saves mark ever, just seven shy of his personal high-water mark set in 1998.

B. Although he is missing one kidney, it didn't slow him down—he was the reigning all-time saves king, exiting his career with 601, later to be usurped by Mariano Rivera. The man in question registered many of his saves using a change-up rather than, say, a heater that so many closers such as Billy Wagner could bring.

C. In 1998, when he recorded 53 saves and blew just one, it was good for a then-record 98.1 percent save conversion rate. As an aside, his wife used to be a cheerleader for the Buffalo Bills.

NAME THAT BALLPLAYER

61 A. This pitcher, last active in 2008 with Milwaukee after establishing his stellar credentials with the Dodgers, had a save conversion rate of 100 percent in 2003, and his 55 saves tied the NL record. That same year 55 percent of the outs he recorded came on strikeouts. Further, over a stretch of nearly two years, he ran up a record streak of 84 saves before he blew one.

   B. When he entered a game in LA, the stadium's message screens proclaimed GAME OVER, while the song "Welcome to the Jungle" blared over the PA. In 2003, he became the first pitcher to win the Cy Young Award with a losing record (2–3).

   C. On June 6, 2006, he and his catcher, Russell Martin, hooked up to become the first-ever French Canadian–born battery mates.

62 A. He was famous for the expression, "Hit 'em where they ain't." In 1897 he compiled a 44-game hitting streak, the same length as Pete Rose's modern-day NL record. The next year he collected 206 *singles*.

   B. According to the Hall of Fame website, this man "used one of the shortest, yet heaviest bats in major league history, just 30 inches long but weighing 46 ounces." He wielded it well, slashing 200+ hits a record eight years running. He was such an effective bunter, baseball officials drew up the rule decreeing that a foul bunt with two strikes was an automatic strikeout.

   C. His nickname, due to his diminutive stature (around 5-foot-4 and 140 pounds), was "Wee Willie."

63 A. Surprisingly, this man—who won three Cy Young Awards, all unanimously and all back in the day when only one such award was presented in the majors each year—fired four no-hitters (one a perfect game), and won an MVP Award, yet only got the honor of the starting nod on Opening Day once, in 1964.

   B. He ended up a cinch for the Hall of Fame, yet struggled with his control in his early days with the Brooklyn Dodgers.

   C. In two of his Cy Young seasons he won the pitchers' Triple Crown, and he led the NL in ERA every year from 1962 through

1966. His 382 strikeouts in 1965 was the single-season record until Nolan Ryan surpassed that mark.

64 A. A former Yankees captain, this Gold Glove third baseman appeared in 2,700 contests from 1967 through 1988, more than any other player who did not take part in a no-hitter.

B. His nickname was "Puff," and he truly was adept at pulling off pranks and then disappearing so as not to get caught. He was also great when it came to one-liners, like this one about Sparky Lyle: "He went from Cy Young to sayonara in a year."

C. He set the AL record for lifetime homers by a third baseman (390), helped the Yanks win four pennants, and made the highlight reel for his defense in the 1978 World Series.

65 A. As great as this Dodgers star was (407 HR), during a golden era of baseball, he was only the third-best center fielder in New York, behind Willie Mays and Mickey Mantle.

B. He is an eight-time All-Star and a Hall of Famer. One of the "Boys of Summer," he hit the last homer ever at Ebbets Field. He hit four homers in the 1952 and the 1955 World Series, and his 11 lifetime Series homers is the best among non-Yankees.

C. The "Duke of Flatbush" had his jersey (#4) retired by the Dodgers in 1980.

66 A. When he hit 28 homers in 2006, this man and his father, Cecil, became just the third father-son duo to record seasons with 25+ HR, joining the Bonds combo and Felipe and Moises Alou. In 2007 he exploded for 50 homers, one shy of his father's career high.

B. He broke in with Milwaukee in 2005 but was still (officially) a rookie in 2006.

C. His first name—and it *is* his real name—is also a term usually associated with royalty.

67 A. This slugger, whose concept of the strike zone was "any pitch I can reach," was a lifetime .318 hitter. He hit .300 or better every full season he played in the majors since 1997 when he broke in with the Expos.

B. On defense, this right fielder's forte was his outstanding arm.

C. In 2004 he took home the AL MVP Award. He and his brother Wilton were teammates for several years in Montreal. He was inducted into the Hall of Fame in 2018, one year before his son earned his own headlines by enjoying a fine rookie season.

68 A. A Yankee great, this 5-foot-10 southpaw is reportedly the only post–World War II pitcher to stand less than 6 feet tall and make it to the Hall of Fame.

B. Only five men had a better won-loss percentage than his lifetime stratospheric .690, and among pitchers with 200+ decisions (not counting active players), he ranks first in that realm. In 1961 he won the Cy Young Award, and, after beating Babe Ruth's record for the most consecutive shutout innings in the World Series, he was named the Series MVP.

C. "The Chairman of the Board" was also known for his rollicking times with drinking buddies Mickey Mantle and Billy Martin.

69 A. Known as "Boomer," he twice led his league in total bases and won eight Gold Gloves.

B. This first baseman didn't use his middle initial, which is "C," but he shares his name with the actor who played the title role in the movie *Patton*.

C. He is best remembered for his days with the Brewers and the Red Sox.

70 A. He's generally regarded as the greatest fielding third baseman ever.

B. All 23 of his big league seasons were spent with the Orioles, a longevity record for an entire career with one club.

C. His scintillating play in the 1970 World Series earned him the MVP. He was the AL MVP in 1964 as well.

71 A. He was the second African American to break the color barrier and the second African-American to manage a big league club. In addition, in both cases the man he followed was named Robinson (Jackie and Frank, respectively). He was also the second African American to play in Japan's Nippon

Professional Baseball league, this time preceded by Don Newcombe.

B. He was with the Indians for most of his career and played on both the world champion squad of 1948 and the pennant-winning team of 1954. The '54 Tribe steamrolled its way to an American League record of 111 wins in the regular season, only to be swept by Willie Mays and the Giants in the World Series.

C. Quickie clues: His first name is Larry, he led his league in homers and RBI in '54, he was an outfielder, and he was inducted into the Hall of Fame in 1998.

72 A. This Hall of Famer toiled 300 or more innings six years running, led the NL in complete games five years in a row, and, from 1952 through 1954, averaged almost 30 complete games a year.

B. He was a member of the 500-home-run club in that he served up an all-time record 505 homers over his 19-year career, spent mainly with the Phillies.

C. A member of the "Whiz Kids" who won the 1950 NL pennant, he won 20 that year, and went on to capture 286 victories in all.

73 A. Both he and his brother Lloyd (a.k.a., "Little Poison") are in the Hall of Fame, making for a very venomous duo.

B. Most of his 20 seasons and most of his 3,152 hits came with him in the uniform of the Pirates.

C. He was the 1927 NL MVP who led Pittsburgh to the pennant. Unfortunately, those Pirates were swept by the Murderers' Row Yankees. In fact, legend has it that the Pirates were finished the moment they watched the Yankees crash pitch after pitch out of spacious Forbes Field in batting practice *before* the Series even began.

74 A. The 2005 season was the breakthrough one for this Phillies infielder, who finished 13th in MVP balloting that year.

B. He followed that up by rattling off three seasons in which he produced 40 or more doubles and he swatted 30+ homers in three of his next four seasons. He even strung together four straight seasons with 100 or more RBIs, and only three other second basemen have won more than his four Silver Slugger Awards.

C. As a verb, his first name is something effective batters like this man seldom do with bad pitches.

75 A. This Hall of Fame pitcher was nothing short of dazzling in the 1970s, the decade in which he won all three of his Cy Young Awards. His entire career spanned the years from 1965 through 1984, and he spent each of those seasons with the same club, the Baltimore Orioles.

B. He won 268 career contests at a .638 won-loss clip, and with eight 20-win seasons in all. Three times he led the AL in wins, twice in ERA, and he even took home four Gold Glove Awards.

C. Despite all of his accomplishments, if one played the word-association game and was asked to respond to this man's name, the reply might well be "underwear model." However, he was also famous for his running feud with legendary O's manager Earl Weaver.

○ ○ ○ **1** ○ ○ ○

ANSWERS

1 Nolan Ryan. He also holds the all-time high for walks surrendered and wild pitches unleashed. Additionally, and not at all surprisingly, for his final four seasons he was the oldest player in the game. He even fanned 157 men over 157 ⅓ innings in his next-to-last season, at the age of 45. Plus, he's number-one all-time at holding opponents to the lowest batting average, a meager .204.

2 Barry Zito. At the time he signed his pact, only Alex Rodriguez, Derek Jeter, Manny Ramirez, Todd Helton, and Alfonso Soriano held contracts worth more guaranteed loot than Zito, who took part in baseball's 14th $100+ million deal—four of them coming in the 2006 off-season.

3 Joe DiMaggio. While most fans know about his marvelous hitting streak, few know that he owns the modern-day record for the most RBI in a month—he drove home 53 runs in August of 1939, the year he wound up with "only" 126 runs batted in.

4 Willie Mays. Trivia: He holds the record for the longest gap between MVP wins—11 seasons. He won in 1954 and then again in 1965. Barry Bonds first won an MVP in 1990 and copped his last one in 2004, but never went as many years in between two MVP seasons as Mays did.

5. Cy Young. Incredibly, when the results for the inaugural election for the Hall of Fame were announced on February 2, 1936, Young, who owned almost 100 wins more than any other pitcher, was picked on just half of all ballots. Five men were inducted as charter members of the Hall, even though voters were permitted to select as many as ten players. Astonishingly, men such as Young, Tris Speaker, Rogers Hornsby, and Nap Lajoie were initially denied Fame recognition.

6. David Eckstein

7. Ty Cobb. No man had more hits than his 3,900 for one team, the Tigers. Also, on 13 occasions Cobb hit 100 or more points higher than his league's average.

8. Mickey Mantle. He hit with tornadic force, and his 536 lifetime shots rank 15th on the all-time list through 2008.

9. Joe Mauer of the Twins. The last catcher before him to win a batting crown was Ernie Lombardi, way back in 1942 when he hit .330 for the Boston Braves. What made that so astonishing is that he was *very* slow on the bases, nearly as immobile as a traffic pylon.

10. Scott Rolen

11. Jason Schmidt

12. Tris Speaker. His shallow positioning helped allow him to smash records for outfield assists and putouts. Further, he still owns marks for the most double plays turned in by a center fielder, 135; and his 450 career and 35 (AL) assists in a season (done twice) are also records.

13. Bruce Sutter, one of only a handful of relievers to win the Cy Young Award.

14. Joe Niekro

15. Manny Ramirez. Another strange incident involving Ramirez (or, as such moments have come to be known, "Manny being Manny") came on July 21, 2004, when, unbelievably, and in an unprecedented play, Ramirez cut off a throw from

center fielder Johnny Damon. The throw was intended to hold Baltimore's David Newhan to a triple, but due to Ramirez's lapse, Newhan wound up with an inside-the-park homer.

16 Rod Carew

17 Stan "The Man" Musial

18 Ken Griffey Jr. Although Donora is a small town, it also produced several other big leaguers, including Steve Filipowicz, who also played pro football, plus Dan Towler, who led the NFL in rushing once.

19 Lou Gehrig. An odd and little-known fact about his streak of consecutive games played: His first appearance to launch his longevity skein came when he pinch-hit for Pee-Wee Wanninger. The irony here is that earlier that season, Wanninger had taken the starting shortstop job away from Everett Scott, to break *his* record streak of 1,307 straight games played. Thus, Gehrig (as a pinch hitter) replaced Wanninger, who had, in turn, replaced the man who had held the mark for the most consecutive games before Gehrig eventually shot by him. The next day "The Iron Horse" filled in for Wally Pipp, ailing from his now-famous headache after being hit by a batting-practice pitch, at first base, never to lose that job until his own, much more serious, illness snapped his stupendous streak. By the way, Aaron and Mathews wound up with 863 combined homers as teammates.

20 Frank Thomas

21 Alex Rodriguez

22 Pete Rose, a.k.a., "Charlie Hustle." He hung up his spikes only after he ripped 4,256 hits, including 3,215 total singles, to breeze by Cobb's old records of 4,191 lifetime hits and 3,053 singles. However, the ominous cloud of gambling charges has left Rose banished from Hall of Fame consideration thus far.

23 Rafael Palmeiro

24 Chipper Jones

25 Carl Hubbell

26 Miguel Cabrera

27 Ron Guidry. Oddity: All three of his losses in 1978 came to left-handers, each with the first name of Mike—Caldwell, Flanagan, and Willis.

28 Mark "The Bird" Fidrych. A non-roster invitee to spring training in 1974, he made the team when the Tigers broke camp, but got his initial start about six weeks into the season only when the regularly scheduled pitcher was scratched from the lineup due to the flu. In his debut, he worked no-hit ball for seven innings, went the distance on two hits, and secured a 2–1 nail-biter. Once before throwing the first pitch of a road game, he looked down and noticed the grounds crew had scattered birdseed over the mound.

29 Jimmie Foxx. In 1934, some felt Foxx deserved a third consecutive MVP, but Detroit's Mickey Cochrane of the pennant-winning Tigers (managed by Cochrane) won it with two homers to Foxx's 44, and just 76 RBIs to 130 for Foxx. It seems that, at times, he was denied some of the respect he deserved. For instance, in 1932, although he was headed for an MVP trophy, he did not make an appearance in the All-Star Game. He did wind up being the first man to win the MVP three times. Incidentally, the season Foxx nearly won a Triple Crown, his .364 batting average was a mere three points shy of Dale Alexander.

30 Andruw Jones

31 Bob Feller. At the age of 17, "Rapid Robert" once struck out 17 batters in a game; only he and Kerry Wood, with his 20 whiffs versus Houston on May 6, 1998, ever had a single game strikeout total which matched their ages.

32 Honus Wagner

33 Tim Raines. In 1983 he set an NL record when he scored almost 20 percent (.196, to be exact) of his Expos' total runs on the year. Burt Shotton of the 1913 St. Louis Browns (at .199) holds the all-time high.

34 Ron LeFlore

35 Gary Matthews Jr.

36 Johnny Damon

37 Adam Dunn. Quick aside: In 2004 he lifted a Jose Lima pitch that traveled about 535 feet, left the Great American Ball Park, and eventually came to a stop on a piece of driftwood on the neighboring Ohio River. One source said that this home run may have been the first ever to cross a state line while in the air.

38 Roy Campanella

39 Gary Sheffield

40 Phil Niekro. His "pitch du jour" when he won #300—for that matter, his pitch of *every* day—was, of course, his knuckleball. Trivia note: Among all pitchers who wound up with 300+ wins, Niekro owned the fewest by the time he turned 30, just 31 victories, some 43 wins less than the former record holder, the ageless Gaylord Perry. Also, his 300th win was a shutout, making him the oldest man to blank an opponent.

41 Dizzy Dean

42 Greg Maddux. In 1994, Maddux was the first pitcher to boast of an ERA two runs or lower than every team in his league (1.56).

43 Roy Oswalt

44 Frank Robinson. What a high school sports factory he attended in Oakland, California (McClymonds High)—he played baseball alongside future big league stars Vada Pinson and Curt Flood, and was a member of the basketball team that also boasted future NBA Hall of Famer Bill Russell. The school also produced such luminaries as track star Jim Hines; NBA players Joe Ellis, Antonio Davis, Nate Williams, and Paul Silas; and rapper MC Hammer.

45 Miguel Tejada. According to *USA Today Sports Weekly*, in early April of 2007 Tejada, at 5-foot-9, was then the shortest cleanup hitter in baseball.

46 David Wells

47 David Cone

48 Babe Ruth. Many fans either don't realize that Ruth, whose pitching career shone with klieg-light brightness, posted a career ERA of 2.28, had a staggering won-loss percentage of .671, hit .342 lifetime, and even stole 123 bases to go with his 136 career triples. Not only that, when he retired, his home-run total was more than double the amount of the next slugger on the all-time list, Lou Gehrig, and only Ruth, Gehrig, and Hornsby, with 300 on the nose, had, at that time, reached the 300-homer level.

49 Ted Williams. Additional trivia: Of all the men in the 500-home-run circle, Williams boasts the highest career batting average, some .002 points above that of Babe Ruth. When Williams refused to sit out the doubleheader at the conclusion of the 1941 season, he commented, "I don't care to be known as a .400 hitter with a lousy average of .39955." According to the excellent Baseball Almanac website, only Williams and Andre Dawson ever connected for home runs against father-son pitching duos. Finally, Williams was robbed of the 1947 MVP trophy when Mel Webb, a Boston writer said to have a grudge against the Red Sox superstar, didn't cast a vote (not even a token tenth-place vote) for "The Splendid Splinter" who put up these numbers: .343, 40 two-base hits, a remarkable .499 on-base percentage, 32 HR, and 114 RBIs. Joe DiMaggio won the MVP *by one point* with these stats: .315, 31 doubles, a .391 on-base percentage, 20 homers, and 97 runs driven in. Webb not awarding a vote to Williams cost "The Splendid Splinter" the trophy. Thus, Williams became the only man to win two Triple Crowns and not win the MVP in either of those seasons (Joe Gordon was the MVP in 1942, the year of Williams's first Triple Crown).

50 Carlos Delgado

51 Mike Cameron

52 Ryne "Ryno" Sandberg. A nine-time Gold Glover and a ten-time All-Star, he is the uncle of another big leaguer, Jared Sandberg.

53 Johnny Bench. He was also the youngest player to win his league's MVP Award.

54 Walter Johnson. His 417 win total trails only Cy Young's 511.

55 Roger Clemens. He is the oldest man to win an ERA title (1.87 in 2005 at the age of 43), and he was the first pitcher ever to hit the 20-win plateau with just one defeat, doing that in 2001.

56 Yogi Berra

57 Joe Jackson

58 Curt Schilling

59 Gaylord Perry. Trivia note: The only other time pitchers from two teams threw no-hitters in back-to-back games during a series was in 1969, when Jim Maloney of the Reds and Houston's Don Wilson did it. Interestingly, one player, Bobby Tolan, appeared in all four of these unusual no-hitters.

60 Trevor Hoffman. During his career, he commented on his style and speed, saying he once threw "in the mid-90s, and now I'm in, roughly, the mid-80s, upper-80s on some good days." To throw so "slow" and be so effective is rare.

61 Eric Gagne

62 Willie Keeler

63 Sandy Koufax. He was also the only pitcher to win the Cy Young Award in his final season. For trivia lovers: The same man, Harvey Kuenn, made the last out in Koufax's second no-hitter and in his perfect game.

64 Graig Nettles

65 Duke Snider

66 Prince Fielder

67 Vladimir Guerrero

68 Whitey Ford

69 George Scott

70 Brooks Robinson. The human vacuum cleaner remains the consensus choice as the greatest glove ever at the hot corner.

71 Larry Doby

72 Robin Roberts. He also held the record for the most home runs given up in a single season, until another pitcher (who will be the answer to a question in a subsequent chapter) came along.

73 Paul Waner

74 Chase Utley

75 Jim Palmer. In the 1966 World Series the Orioles absolutely neutralized the Dodgers. Los Angeles scored two runs in the first game of the Series, with the second of those runs coming in the last half of the third inning. The next game featured Palmer blanking the Dodgers, and, when two more shutouts followed, the Orioles had run up a World Series record by firing 33 ⅔ straight whitewash innings against the impotent Dodgers bats. The O's staff also set records by allowing only two runs, a mere 17 hits, the fewest amount of total bases (23), and the lowest team batting average (.142) for a Series of any duration. In short, they dominated the shell-shocked Dodgers.

$\circ \circ \circ$ **2** $\circ \circ \circ$

THE EARLY INNINGS

1 A. This left-handed power hitter, a member of the 500-home-run club, was once involved in a brawl at third base, his position, with Frank Robinson. Robinson had complained that the man in question applied a tag on him with too much force. The third-baseman hauled off and slugged Robinson, then asked, "How about *that* tag?"

B. A teammate of Hank Aaron's for many years, he later managed Aaron.

C. This Hall of Famer has the initials "E.M."

2 A. Along with Mickey Mantle, this man made up the "M and M Boys" of the Yankees.

B. Not many big leaguers come out of North Dakota, but he did (actually, he was born in Minnesota, and then moved to Fargo as a youth).

C. Two words say it all here: 61 homers.

3 A. Along with Willie Mays, the Giants had their own "M" duo of sluggers; the man in question this time was their first baseman and, at 6-foot-4, was known as "Stretch." Wearing his familiar number 44 across his broad shoulders, he propelled 521 home runs.

B. Nicknamed "Big Mac," he spent all but three of his 22 seasons with San Francisco.

C. He was so popular in the Bay Area, the Giants' current ballpark has an area beyond right field, where "splash-down" homers land with a resounding *ker-plunk*, named after him.

4 A. Like Hank Aaron (and a few other huge major league stars), this man was born in Mobile, Alabama, and like Aaron was a slugger with more than 500 home runs to his credit.

B. He began his career as a smooth shortstop before converting to first base.

C. His enthusiasm for the game was his trademark, as was his famous saying, "Let's play two!"

5 A. Weighing three pounds at birth, this outfielder, who broke into the majors in 1991 and lasted through 2007, is a big league tumbleweed. Since 2002, he never stayed with a club longer than one year. In 2007 he played for his 11th team, tying Todd Zeile for the most clubs played for by a position player.

B. Greyhound-quick, he notched 60 or more stolen bases four times during his career, and owns 622 career steals. He has also used his speed to cover center field, sometimes employing a burst of speed to overcome a lapse in reading the ball off the bat.

C. In his first stint with Cleveland, he led the American League in steals each year from 1992 through 1996. From 1995 through 2007, he appeared in postseason play every year but two.

6 A. Another item about a speedster: This man actually holds the mark for the most times being caught stealing in a single season, as he was gunned down 42 times in 1982.

B. Nevertheless, he is an all-time great, a run-producing machine who is also universally considered to be the best hitter ever in the position he normally held down in the batting order.

C. An outfielder by trade, he was an eight-cylinder engine in a four-cylinder world; he ran full throttle, he ran superbly, and he ran often. During the same season that he established the futility record for being caught stealing, he also set the all-time high for stolen bases when he swiped 130 bases in all.

7 A. This man had about as much power as the 1997 flood of the mighty Mississippi. He even threatened to usurp Mickey Mantle as the most prolific switch-hitter, but fell short, with 504 career homers to 536 for "The Mick."

B. A Hall of Famer, inducted in 2003 in his first year of eligibility, he was as steady as a metronome: He walloped 25 or more homers a dozen times, but never topped 33 in a single season. His brother, named Rich, had two sips of coffee at the major league level.

C. The man in question played 2,413 games at first base, the most ever in major league history, and is one of three men (along with Hank Aaron and Willie Mays) to hit more than 500 home runs with 3,000+ hits.

8 A. This man is a member of the 2007 Class for the Hall of Fame, not only gaining admittance on his first try, but also earning the highest percentage of votes (98.53 percent; only eight voters did not select him) for a non-pitcher in the history of baseball. That percentage was later surpassed by Ken Griffey, Jr., and among pitchers, by Mariano Rivera when he was a unanimous selection.

B. This popular star is best remembered as a shortstop, but moved to third late in his career (1981–2001), which was spent entirely with one franchise.

C. At one point this two-time MVP (1983 and 1991) played under his father. Starting with the year after he was named the AL Rookie of the Year, he made the All-Star squad every season of his career.

9 A. Only this player and Lou Gehrig (in 1939) were admitted into the Hall of Fame without having to wait out the required five seasons before being eligible for induction.

B. Even though he was a four-time batting champ—all of his crowns coming in the 1960s—he is equally remembered for his defensive play, especially for his cannon of an arm, and his full-tilt, racehorse ways on the base paths.

C. He won the NL MVP in 1966 but somehow escaped lavish national attention, despite his fantastic outfield play (12 Gold Gloves, tied with Willie Mays for the most ever by an outfielder). This all changed when he was spotlighted in the 1971 World Series against Baltimore, where he displayed his skills and hit a lusty .414.

10 A. This NL outfielder racked up 3,141 lifetime hits, many by going the opposite way with his magic wand of a bat—he absolutely feasted on pitches middle of the plate and out.

B. A 15-time All-Star, he also won five Gold Gloves, hit for a stunning .338 lifetime average, and tied Honus Wagner's league record by claiming eight batting titles.

C. He never hit as many as 20 home runs in a single season, but he accumulated more than 1,000 RBIs and was a perennial .300+ hitter.

11 A. This player was the recipient of a "gift" home run when a young fan, Jeffrey Maier, interfered with the play of Orioles outfielder Tony Tarasco on October 9, 1996, during Game 1 of the American League Championship Series, but umpires ruled there had been no interference.

B. The player in question won the Rookie of the Year Award in 1996.

C. He also won the Gold Glove as the top shortstop in the AL in 2004, 2005, and 2006.

12 A. He's one of only three players in the Hall of Fame—he was inducted in 1999 after playing from 1974 through 1993—with the last initial of "Y."

B. He played his entire 20-year career with the same club but manned several positions, including a handful of games at first base and as his team's designated hitter. However, the bulk of his career was spent at shortstop early on, and then in the outfield.

C. He was the AL MVP in both 1982 and 1989.

13 A. He broke into the majors in 1926 as a 17-year-old, and spent his full 22-year career with the same NL club. He is the only player ever to score six runs in a game on two occasions.

B. This man is one of just two players enshrined in the Hall of Fame and *the* only modern-era player in the Hall whose last initial is "O."

C. He is probably best known for his 511 lifetime home runs and his unique batting style.

14 A. This scrappy catcher was an AL All-Star in 2003, 2005, and 2008, representing his Eastern Division team.

B. He suffered through a miserable World Series in 2004 when he hit just .154, but he didn't mind *too* much, as that was the year his team pounced back from a three-games-to-none deficit in the ALCS to claim the pennant before sweeping the Cardinals in the World Series.

C. One of his most famous, or infamous, moments on the diamond took place when he shoved his mitt into Alex Rodriguez's face during a brawl between the rival Red Sox and Yankees.

15 A. This outfielder, usually seen roaming right field, was a teammate of the man in question above from 1998 through 2006, but, unlike that teammate—who played for one team exclusively—this man played with a new club, the Indians, and spent a brief time with the Mets in 2008.

B. He was a first-round draft pick in 1993, hit .274 lifetime, and is considered to be a hard-nosed player who places winning above personal statistics.

C. His first name is a synonym for the word "run," while his last name is the same as that of a former president of the United States.

16 A. This man pitched for, among other teams, the San Francisco Giants, the Washington Nationals, and the Arizona Diamondbacks. He is also the half brother of another pitcher who has been with both the New York Yankees and Mets.

B. Both men defected from Cuba and became stars in the majors.

C. The man in question was a member of the 1997 World Series champs and won the MVP that year for both the NLCS and the World Series (he went 2–0 in both series). One of the perks that came to him was being named the grand marshal for the Orange Bowl parade that year.

17 A. This outfielder with the initials "J.C." was a steady, very productive outfielder (396 HR) from 1983 through 1998, playing for six teams, with his longest stint coming with the Blue Jays.

B. One of the most dramatic home runs of all time came when he drove a Mitch Williams pitch in the World Series of 1993 for a walk-off homer. With his Blue Jays down 6–5, he came to the plate in a situation where the Phillies were just two outs shy of forcing a Game 7. He changed all of that with what became his famous Series-clinching blast.

C. This man was traded, in a multiplayer package, from Cleveland to the Padres for Chris James, Carlos Baerga, and Sandy Alomar Jr., and later would be packaged with Sandy's brother Roberto in a move that sent him from San Diego to Toronto for Fred McGriff and Tony Fernandez.

18 A. A Hall of Fame catcher, inducted in 2003, he played from 1974 through 1992, gaining most of his fame first in Montreal, and then with the New York Mets. Twice he flirted with the NL MVP Award, but fell a bit short both times.

B. The Hall of Fame website calls him a "rugged receiver and enthusiastic on-field general." He excelled on both offense and defense, catching in 2,056 contests, drilling 324 home runs, and driving in 1,225 runs.

C. In a rarity, he won the MVP trophy in two All-Star contests, in 1981 and again three years later.

19 A. He is one of the greatest second basemen ever, having won more Gold Gloves (ten) than any other second sacker while also hitting a ton. From 1988 through 2004, he hit .300 lifetime with 2,724 hits, 210 homers, and more than 1,000 runs driven in.

B. His father and brother, both named Sandy, were big leaguers. As a matter of fact, his brother and he became the first brother act to win All-Star game MVPs.

C. Unfortunately for this heady and multitalented player, he is often remembered for an incident in which he spat on umpire John Hirschbeck in 1996.

20 A. Although this outfielder didn't get a lot of national ink—largely because he languished on poor Pittsburgh teams from his first full season in 2004 through most of the 2008 season, when he was dealt away—he did become the first Pirate in the franchise's long, illustrious history to win the Rookie of the Year Award.

B. He is a Canadian product, born in British Columbia, and represented Canada in the initial World Baseball Classic in 2006. He also played for Canada in the 1990 Little League World Series. Furthermore, he was drafted by the Montreal Expos, but broke into the majors, briefly, with the Padres before settling down in Pittsburgh.

C. His sister Lauren, a professional softball player, pitched for the Canadian team in the 2004 Olympics, and one of his friends, Shawn Horcoff, a former center for the Edmonton Oilers, is also from his hometown.

21 A. This Hall of Famer's power made him a real "killer" of opposing pitchers. In 1963 his 45 home runs became a single-season high for a batter who did *not* drive in 100 or more runs.

B. He pelted more home runs than any right-handed American Leaguer ever, 573, playing from 1954, when he entered the majors with the old Washington Senators, through 1975.

C. Most fans recall him as a member of the Minnesota Twins who played first, third, and a bit in the outfield. Few remember that he actually played 11 games at second base over his first few seasons.

22 A. Perhaps the greatest hitting catcher ever, this man won the Silver Slugger Award in his first full season, 1993, and continued to win that honor for the next nine years running.

B. Though his arm was very suspect, he does own the record for the most lifetime homers hit by a catcher—396.

C. He could hit for average, too, with his .308 lifetime mark and his personal high of .362 serving as testimony. His .362 zenith, virtually unheard of for a catcher (only he and Bill Dickey ever hit that high), came with his initial team, the Dodgers.

23 A. This man's largest claim to greatness comes from his mound magic, but he also holds the standard for the most career home runs hit by an NL pitcher, hitting 35 in all, all with the Boston/Milwaukee franchise.

B. To this day, no southpaw has won as many games as this man (363). Consider, too, that it's impossible to say how many additional wins he would have come through with had the Buffalo, New York, native not spent time in the United States Army. He served in Europe where he earned a Purple Heart and a Bronze Star for bravery. He had not a full cup, but a mere swig of big league coffee in 1942, and would not toe the rubber again in the majors until 1946 (in just 24 contests).

C. His second no-hitter came after his 40th birthday; it's obvious that this was one durable hurler. In fact, through 2019 only four modern-era legends—Cy Young, Walter Johnson, Grover Cleveland Alexander, and Christy Mathewson—won more games than this man.

24 A. Prior to 2000, this man was the only player to ever produce a season in which extra base hits accounted for 60 percent or more of his total hits. In 1999, of his 145 hits, he had 21 doubles, one triple, and 65 homers.

B. Looking at his size now, it may seem surprising that he won an AL Gold Glove in 1990 as a first baseman.

C. His name was stained due to the steroid controversy; his testimony before a congressional panel turned him into an instant pariah, and cost him many a Hall of Fame vote in 2007 (he was never named on more than 23.7 percent of the ballots while he was eligible). Still, his 583 homers places him 11th on the all-time list.

25 A. Lee Smith, baseball's all-time save king (until Trevor Hoffman, and later Mariano Rivera breezed by him), said this slugger had "some of the quickest and strongest hands I've ever seen on a hitter." In fact, his blend of power and defense at one of the corners of the infield made him the greatest ever at his position.

B. Sure, Brooks Robinson, with a sensational glove and 16 Gold Gloves (most ever for *any* position other than pitcher) was spectacular, but this man hit exactly the same average as Robinson, at .267; won ten Gold Gloves, second most by a third baseman; and tossed in 548 homers to Robinson's 268.

C. He came to Philadelphia in 1972, out of Ohio University, and spent his entire 18 years in the majors with the Phillies.

26 A. This outfielder often took a sort of lunging swing which sometimes actually featured him running up on the ball and towards first base. With his defensive-back speed, if a bounding ball hit in the infield—sometimes just once—an infielder had little chance of throwing him out. From 2001 through 2008 he put up 100+ runs, 200+ hits, 30 or more steals, and hit over .300 every single year.

B. Hitting aside, this man, so famous and recognizable he's often referred to by his first name only, is a defensive whiz. Since he came to this country and entered the majors in 2001 he lugged home a Gold Glove Award annually through 2010.

C. He was a lifetime .311 hitter who, amazingly, bettered George Sisler's old record for the most hits in a season (257 in 1920) when he laced 262 hits in 2004.

27 A. Not too many men have been as versatile as this Houston great, who has been an All-Star as a catcher once (in 1991), and as a second baseman six times. Then, later in his career

in 2003, he became a full-time center fielder, and played both left and center the following season, before returning to second in 2005. He was still at second in his final season, 2007, as a 41-year-old, but, for sentimental reasons, played two innings behind the plate that year.

B. Rickey Henderson tops them all when it comes to hitting the most lifetime home runs to lead off games (with 81), but this man has hit the most such shots in NL play.

C. More than just a shared last initial "B" links this man with fellow Astros star Jeff Bagwell. For a baseball eon, from 1991 through 2005, these men were teammates who were "lethal" to opponents.

28 A. He is most remembered for his ability to lash out line drives as forceful as a Dick Butkus forearm smash.

B. He could do it all. He hit .305 lifetime and ranks as number three on the all-time hit list, and he's first for career total bases, extra base hits, and RBIs, averaging 100 per year for 23 seasons!

C. Powerful, yes, but he won two batting titles as well with his 1959 crown representing his highest season average ever, at a blistering .355.

29 A. In 2003, when the Cubs seemed to have secured a trip to the World Series, leading the Marlins 3–0 with a mere five outs to go in Game 6 of the NLCS, a fan named Steve Bartman (not to be confused with the name of a dance on *The Simpsons*) got in the way of this left fielder, preventing him from making a catch. After that, the floodgates opened, Florida scored eight runs, and the next night the Cubs fell after surrendering a 5–3 lead.

B. During a game in 2006, Barry Bonds, Steve Finley, and this player comprised the oldest outfield in big league history, with each player being over 40 years of age.

C. He hit .321 for Florida against the Indians when the Marlins won the 1997 World Series.

30 A. In a related question, this man was pitching for Chicago the night of the notorious Bartman Incident.

B. This University of Southern California star was plagued with injuries which prevented him from living up to his early laudatory press clippings.

C. He went 18–6 in 2003 to compliment his lustrous 2.43 ERA. Subsequently, he went 6–4, 11–7, and 1–6 with an inflated 7.21 ERA in 2006.

31 A. In 1964, he was involved in a trade, going from the Cubs, along with several other players, to the Cardinals for Ernie Broglio, Bobby Shantz, and a few throw-ins. It may have been the most lopsided deal since the Lenape Indian tribe was fleeced in what amounted to a $24 swap for the island of Manhattan (with their chief, Tammany, being the equivalent of the Cubs general manager). The player in question went on to the Hall of Fame, while Broglio won seven games over his 2 ½ seasons as a Cub, and Shantz went 0–1 in Chicago.

B. For years this outfielder's name was synonymous with speed: He led the NL in stolen bases eight times, established a single-season high of 118 bases stolen in 1974, and now stands second on the all-time steals list behind Rickey Henderson.

C. Although he is a member of the 3,000-hit club, he is one of just a few members not to sport a .300+ lifetime batting average (.293).

32 A. When the man who is the answer to the above question played in the fifth game of the 1968 World Series, one key play involved him somehow neglecting to slide home on what was seemingly a potential bang-bang play. His decision to go in standing up cost the Cardinals dearly, as Detroit rallied shortly after he was tagged out by this Tigers catcher. Thus, the play, many felt, proved to be a turning point in that Fall Classic.

B. This man, a five-time Gold Glove winner, was such a fine defensive player that the Rawlings sporting goods company listed him as one of five catchers on their 2007 ballot for their

47

All-Time Gold Glove Team, along with Johnny Bench, Ivan Rodriguez, Jim Sundberg, and Bob Boone.

C. Over his 15 seasons, all spent in the Tigers uniform, he hit 200 home runs, then good for the third-best power production ever by a catcher (topped only by Yogi Berra and Bill Dickey).

33 A. The year 1924 belonged to this Hall of Fame second baseman. He hit a modern-day NL record of .424 for a season. For that matter, he was so swelteringly hot in the early 1920s that he actually maintained a .402 batting average over a five-year span (1921–25)! Over that ungodly period he hit .397, .401, .384, .424, and .403.

B. He won the Triple Crown in 1922 and 1925, making him the first of only two men (Ted Williams being the other) to win that coveted crown twice. He remains the only player to hit .400+ and rip 40 or more homers in the same season (1922). Only Ty Cobb owns a higher lifetime batting average than this man's .358.

C. His nickname was "The Rajah," but his real first name was given to him, according to the Wikipedia website, to honor his mother's maiden name.

34 A. A big league first took place on September 27, 1998, when Cincinnati fielded an all-sibling infield. Aaron Boone was at third base for the Reds and his brother Bret manned second. The man in question was, as usual, at short while his brother played first.

B. A perennial All-Star and a standout glove, he attended Moeller High School in Cincy, which also produced, among others, Buddy and David Bell, as well as Ken Griffey Jr. In 1997 he began a successful tenure as the Reds team captain.

C. Hugely popular in the Queen City, where he played his full career, he won the 1995 MVP and piled up 2,340 hits before he retired in 2004.

35 A. Few men have a résumé which includes a perfect game, but this hurler achieved that feat on July 28, 1994, while he was with the Texas Rangers.

B. A fine fielder, this man finished his career after the 2008 season with a laudable .584 lifetime won-loss percentage. He was given the nickname "The Gambler" after a song title by a singer who has the same name as this left-hander.

C. In 2006 he made headlines in the postseason for two things: 1) his lights-out pitching—he engineered 23 straight shutout innings; and 2) allegedly cheating (TV cameras displayed a brown-colored substance on his pitching hand). Of course, he had more than his share of volatility and controversy in 2005 when he served a 13-game suspension for shoving two cameramen, nearly putting their lights out.

36 A. Born in 1887 in Nebraska, this all-time great, known as "Old Pete," went on to win a stellar 373 contests, tied for third best ever with Christy Mathewson, and the most wins ever for a pitcher who did not throw a no-hitter.

B. He was hit in the head in 1907 which caused him to suffer from double vision for a few seasons; some feel that this injury was also a factor when he later became epileptic. In 1910 he was fine, but he then made NL hitters ill the following season, his rookie year, when he led the league with 28 wins—still a rookie record.

C. He registered 16 shutouts in 1916, good for another all-time record, had 90 lifetime "whitewash" jobs (#2 all-time), and he won the pitching Triple Crown three times as well. Finally, he was the last pitcher to win 30+ games three years running, from 1915 through 1917.

37 A. He donned the "tools of ignorance" more times than any other catcher, ever: 2,226. Playing seemingly forever, he golfed more home runs while in his 40s than any other man (72).

B. Now in the Hall of Fame, this New Englander played his entire career with the Red, then White Sox. In addition, when he went from Boston to Chicago, he changed uniform numbers by turning the digits of his Red Sox jersey, #27, around, to wear #72 with the White Sox.

C. In 1975 he was involved in one of the most dramatic World Series moments ever.

38 A. Despite hitting 52 doubles with 103 RBIs in 2006, not to mention his lifetime batting average of .300 on the nose, this man remained rather underappreciated (although he did ink a five-year, $80 million contract prior to the 2007 season).

B. When Alfonso Soriano came to Texas in 2004 in exchange for Alex Rodriguez, this man willingly made the defensive switch from second base to shortstop to help his club out.

C. An All-Star from 2004 through 2009, his 858 hits over the 2003 through 2006 span trailed only Ichiro Suzuki.

39 A. This outstanding base burglar, whose career ran from 1976 through 1994, shares his last name with that of an American president—in fact, they both have the same initials, as well.

B. He spent all but his final four seasons with the Kansas City Royals, a team that would go to the playoffs five times with this man in center, reaching the World Series twice and winning it all in 1985.

C. He only led the league in steals once, in his first full season, but posted one of the highest success rates ever. He also won a batting title and was a superb leadoff hitter. On the debit side, in 1983 he pled guilty to a misdemeanor drug charge for attempting to purchase cocaine. He and three other players served jail time for their part in this drug scandal.

40 A. In the 1968 World Series this pitcher dazzled Detroit, whiffing a Series record 17 Tigers.

B. That same season he had also baffled NL hitters all year long with an ERA of 1.12, third lowest in the modern era, going

22–9, while working over 300 "frugal" innings—giving up only 198 hits.

C. "Hoot," or "Gibby," as he was called, was known for his fierce ways, his eyes glaring at batters from just under the bill of his cap.

41 A. The 1968 season truly was "The Year of the Pitcher." That year featured this pitcher becoming the last man to chalk up a 30-win season. No man since Dizzy Dean in 1934 had reached that coveted plateau.

B. He went 31–6 at the age of 24, but lasted only ten years in the majors (131–91 record), retiring from Atlanta after gaining glory with the Tigers.

C. His life was filled with turmoil. There were allegations of bookmaking and of hanging around with known gamblers; he was suspended for carrying a gun on a team flight; and he wound up serving time in prison for embezzlement, drug trafficking, and racketeering.

42 A. This southpaw pitcher, who played from 1995 through 2013, had perhaps the best move to first base of his era, although many opponents claimed he constantly balked.

B. He is a close friend of Roger Clemens, and they pitched together for two different clubs.

C. For his career he won 256 games and had a 19–11 slate in postseason play.

43 A. He played left field as a Chicago teammate of Ernie Banks for an eon.

B. This Whistler, Alabama, product was underrated by many. In 1970 voters gave Johnny Bench the NL MVP plaque, even though this man scored 40 runs more than Bench, collected 28 more hits, and outhit the Reds catcher, .322 to .293. Admittedly, Bench did hit three more homers and drove in 19 more runs, and his team did win the pennant. Still, Bench got 22 of the 24 first-place votes, surprising some experts.

Likewise, in 1972 this star again lost the MVP to Bench after outhitting him, .333 to .270.

C. The "sweet-swingin'" popular Cub now has a flag, sporting his retired jersey number (26), flying from one of Wrigley Field's foul poles in his honor. The Hall of Famer once played in 1,117 consecutive games.

44 A. In March of 2007 this pitcher lamented that he was one of only "two black starters in all of baseball." He won 117 times over his first eight seasons, including 11 victories in 13 decisions over the second half of the 2008 season after being traded. For his new club he logged an incredible 1.65 ERA. He retired after the 2019 season with 251 wins.

B. The local media covering the first team he played for paid much attention to his weight; he was listed between 250 and 290 pounds in 2006, but many suggested he tipped the scales at over 300. They also wrote many words concerning several of his injuries, suggesting they were directly related to his heft. Finally, some have even criticized him for the skewed way he wears his cap—he is a lefty, however, which probably accounts for that idiosyncrasy.

C. His first and middle names are Carsten Charles, but he's certainly not known by those names.

45 A. This man was the *other* 2006 African-American starter, an NL star whose windup and delivery were quite distinctive.

B. Also a lefty, this man was sometimes called "D-train," and his teammates certainly rode him to success in 2005 when he checked in with a shiny 2.63 ERA, went 22–10, and finished second in Cy Young voting. Plus, he was no slouch with the bat—he lifted three homers in 2006, was a lifetime .244 hitter, and, in 2005, became the third modern-day pitcher to rack up 20 wins and 20 hits in a season.

C. It was in 2003 (when he took home the NL Rookie of the Year Award) that his team won the World Series. That postseason, though, he pitched sparingly and not too well. Still, with 58 wins in only four seasons, he was a bona fide star at the age of just 25 going into the 2007 season. That, however, is when things began to turn sour. His record was 10–15 in 2007 before he virtually disappeared in 2008 (0–2, 9.38 ERA). He stuck around through 2011, but after his third season of 2005 he never again had a winning season.

46 A. An outfielder/designated hitter from 1985 through 2001, he won the Rookie of the Year Award in 1986. Then, just two seasons later, he won the AL MVP Award when he created the 40–40 club, coming through with 40+ homers with 40 or more stolen bases.

B. He was born in Havana, Cuba, and his twin brother Ozzie also made it to the big leagues. The player in question was shaky on defense and never lived down a play in which the ball bounded off his head and over the fence for a home run. After his "header," a pro soccer team jokingly offered him a contract. On the offensive side of things, he did demolish 462 balls for homers.

C. He was called a whistleblower for writing an exposé and testifying in Congress about steroid use in baseball.

47 A. Some argue that this man was the greatest—or, at worst, the second-greatest—fielding shortstop ever. He made the routine plays as well as the acrobatic ones and, through 2019, he still held the record for the highest lifetime fielding percentage ever for his position, at a gaudy .985. He once went 95 straight games without committing an error. He won 11 Gold Gloves, two shy of Ozzie Smith, and he won nine of those awards consecutively. He has even turned more double plays than Smith.

B. He and former Cleveland teammate José Mesa had a feud going since the man in question criticized Mesa in his autobiography for blowing the save in Game 7 of the 1997 World Series. A furious Mesa vowed to hit this man with a pitch every time he faced him. After plunking him several times, Mesa finally was suspended for his actions in 2006.

C. He began his career with the M's, but gained much of his attention and glamour with the Indians.

48 A. This reliever, whose specialty pitch was the screwball, coined the phrase "Ya gotta believe!" as the rallying cry for his New York Mets in 1973. It must have worked; the Mets won only 83 regular-season games, but that year it was good enough to thrust them into the playoffs, where they won the pennant but lost the World Series to Oakland.

B. Known as a bit of a flake, one of his most famous lines came when he was asked what he'd do with all the money he was getting paid. He replied with a grin, "Ninety percent I'll spend on good times, women, and Irish whiskey. The other ten percent I'll probably waste." He also developed a syndicated comic strip, appropriately named *Screwball*, which featured a baseball storyline.

C. His son Tim is a huge star in the country music industry.

49 A. This Hall of Famer was called "Hammerin' Hank" years before Hank Aaron came along. In 1935 he led the league in ribbies by a record 51 RBIs over second-ranked Lou Gehrig.

B. A statue of this slugger was erected in his honor at Comerica Park. He established many outstanding records in the Motor City. For instance, in 1937 the two-time MVP absolutely tattooed the ball and drove in runners at a staggering pace of more than one RBI per game, 183 RBIs in all. That total is just one fewer than the all-time AL record set by the venerable Gehrig and is still the third-highest total ever for a season.

C. When he played his final season for the Pirates, a fenced-in part of Forbes Field was nicknamed "_____'s Gardens" for him after the team moved its left-field fence in to take advantage of his power as a pull hitter.

50 A. He was born in Canada, excelled mainly in Chicago with the Cubs, and in Texas, where he posted his career high of 25 vic-

tories. He made it to Cooperstown in 1991 as the first Canadian and as the first member of the 3,000-strikeout club, with fewer than 1,000 walks issued.

B. In the latter part of the 1960s and into the 1970s, he won 20+ games with ho-hum regularity, doing so from 1967 through 1972. His only Cy Young season was 1971, but he finished second or third in the voting four times. It is remarkable that, despite his 284 lifetime wins, he was an All-Star just three times.

C. As a member of the Cubs, he, and later Greg Maddux, wore jersey #31. He first came to the Cubbies in a monumental steal of a deal: The Phillies sent him and two other players, both marginal, for pitchers Larry Jackson and Bob Buhl. Those pitchers went 47–53 with Philadelphia while the pitcher in question paid almost instant dividends, winning 20 games the next season, his first full one as a Cub.

51 A. Sure, playing home games in hitter-friendly Coors Park in Colorado helped boost this man's stats, but make no mistake—he was a hitter. Through 2008, among then-active players, only Albert Pujols and Ichiro Suzuki had a higher lifetime average than his mountainous .328 mark (he ended with a career average of .316). Further, twice he went beyond the 400 strata for total bases. In 2000 he even flirted with the .400 barrier, winding up at .372.

B. Skilled on both offense and defense, he also won three Gold Glove Awards for his play around the first base bag.

C. In 2000 and 2001, he put together back-to-back seasons of 100 or more extra base hits, a big league first. Over his 17-year career he led his league in virtually every significant hitting department.

52 A. As a child, this future star of Los Angeles and San Diego was a batboy for the Dodgers while his father drove a bus for the team in spring training. When the Padres won the 1984 NLCS over the Cubs, this man led the way, hitting a crisp .400. For that, he won his second LCS MVP Award (the other came in 1978 with LA).

B. Wearing his familiar #6 (which the Padres retired), he was a first baseman by trade, but was better known for his offensive productivity; for example, in his NL MVP season, 1974, he hit .312 and drove home 111 runs.

C. His current wife was a key witness in the O. J. Simpson trial. He and his former wife, Cyndy, seemed to have an ideal marriage, but they divorced in 1981, and she later wrote a tell-all book revealing her less-than-flattering version of her husband. His initials are "S.G."

53 A. This Hall of Fame pitcher won 37 games in 1908. Only two American Leaguers, Jack Chesbro and Ed Walsh, ever won more in the modern era.

B. What he did in the 1905 World Series was simply eye-popping. He worked three games, liberally using his specialty pitch, the "fadeaway," won all three, and did so by giving up zero runs over his 27 innings. Plus, he tossed in 18 strikeouts while walking just one batter.

C. The New York Giants great was called "Matty" or "Big Six," and his lifetime ERA of 2.13 is the fourth lowest ever recorded.

54 A. This outfielder, out of USC, was the first rookie to win the MVP Award. Naturally, he also won the Rookie of the Year that season.

B. He copped those trophies in 1975 as a member of the Red Sox, playing alongside Jim Rice and Dwight Evans in one wonderful outfield. Writers dubbed this man and Rice the "Gold Dust Twins."

C. He also played for the Angels and Orioles before making a few late-career pit stops in Detroit and San Diego. Injuries plagued him at times, but he still wound up with just over 300 homers, more than 1,000 runs and RBI, and nearly 2,000 hits. He also owns the first (and through 2019, only) grand slam hit in All-Star competition.

55 A. This pitcher holds the modern record for the highest ERA in a season in which the player had at least ten starts; in 2000

his ERA was a nosebleed-high of 10.64 as opponents hit .357 against him and reached base almost 44 percent of the time.

B. Despite that, he went on to win the Cy Young Award just three years later when his won-loss log read 22–7 and he reduced his ERA to 3.25. Clearly he was able to stand a bit prouder in his Blue Jay uniform that season. He also was a 20-game winner in 2008. In all, he was a 20-game winner three times.

C. In 2006 he boasted a 16–5 mark, good for .762 winning percentage, to lead his league. His real name was Harry Leroy, but he was commonly known as "Doc." By the way, he started his days with the Blue Jays at 21 years of age and was, in fact, the third youngest Toronto pitcher ever to start a game. Final note: he died in Holiday, Florida, in 2017 and the Hall of Fame opened its doors to him two years later.

56 A. Along with Ken Griffey Jr. and Dale Long, this man shares the record for hitting a homer in eight straight games. He did this in July of 1987.

B. A Yankees captain, this popular former first baseman possessed the blend of hitting for both power (442 doubles) and average (.307 lifetime).

C. His nickname was a form of his first name, plus the word "Baseball." Trivia item: Basketball great Larry Bird married his sister. Final clue: He once appeared as a character on *The Simpsons*.

57 A. This intimidating Dodgers great once decided that if he and Sandy Koufax held out together, refusing to sign a contract until both of them were happy with monetary terms—in a sort of unprecedented package deal—they would have more leverage and thus get a fair deal.

B. He is the only pitcher ever to start two All-Star games in one season, doing this in 1959, one of the four seasons baseball held two midsummer classics instead of just one. Three years later he won his only Cy Young Award.

C. This man, who would go on to become a fine baseball announcer, had the nicknames of "Big D" and "Double D." In 1986 he married Ann Myers, a basketball Hall of Famer, making them the first couple both honored by their sport's Hall of Fame.

58 A. A great outfielder with a bazooka for a right arm, this man was the only player to amass 300+ lifetime homers (he had 399) without having once attained 30 home runs.

B. He spent his entire career with the Tigers (1953–74), having never spent a day in the minors.

C. In 1955, he won the batting crown, becoming, at 20, the youngest player ever to accomplish this feat. He never won an MVP and hit just below .300 lifetime, but he compiled 3,007 safeties, was a perennial All-Star, and sailed into the Hall of Fame.

59 A. In the 1989 All-Star Game, this powerful hitter unleashed a monumental homer to dead center, helping him win the MVP Award for that contest.

B. This multisport star out of Auburn was such a powerful hitter that teammates and opponents alike made it a point to observe him during batting practice. He was also the first man to play in a baseball All-Star game as well as in the NFL Pro Bowl.

C. Only he and Vic Janowicz played big league baseball after having earlier earned a Heisman Trophy. Additionally, this man was the first NFL running back to record two touchdowns of 90+ yards.

60 A. After spending some time with the Hiroshima Carp, this man joined the Yankees in 1998 and later played for the Rangers, Nationals, and Cubs before returning to the Yanks to wrap up his career in 2014.

B. He became just the third man to start All-Star games representing both leagues while doing so at different defensive positions. He also hit more homers in a season (13 in 2003) as his team's leadoff batter of the game than any man ever.

C. He began as an infielder and was moved to the outfield in 2005, but not before first balking at the change. Prior to the 2006 season, coming off a great year in which he joined the ritzy 40 HR/40 SB (stolen bases) club (and began a new club by tossing in 40+ doubles), he set a since-broken record for the most money awarded in an arbitration case—$10 million.

61 A. He was the first man to win the Rookie of the Year Award (1949), the Cy Young (in that award's first year of existence, 1956), and the MVP, also in 1956.

B. He was one of the first African American players to make an All-Star squad, joining Larry Doby, Jackie Robinson, and Roy Campanella in 1949.

C. He was on the mound right before Ralph Branca entered the historic 1951 NL playoff game and surrendered the pennant-winning home run to Bobby Thomson.

62 A. This man's first full season was 2005, and he sure grabbed some headlines. He led his NL East team in several categories, hit 27 home runs, drove in 102, and hit .306. He followed that up by hitting .300 or better, with 100 or more RBI in each of the following three seasons.

B. A first-rounder in 2001, he finished as high as fourth in MVP voting in 2007. He did well in the 2006 All-Star Game Home Run Derby, belting out 22 (a mind-reeling 16 in one round, then the third-highest total ever in a single round), but lost anyway. Still, the next day in his first All-Star at bat, he connected off Kenny Rogers.

C. Some say that at one time he and José Reyes formed the best young left side of the infield in baseball. He retired after the 2018 season having played for just one big league team where he become one of the most popular players in that team's history.

63 A. He joined the 300-win club in 2007 and is the fourth-winningest southpaw ever. As a rookie in 1988, however, he led the NL in defeats, going 7–17.

B. A mainstay with the Braves for years, this two-time Cy Young winner joined the Mets in 2003, only to return to Atlanta in 2008.

C. He was the Los Angeles Kings' fourth draft choice, but opted for baseball over hockey. In 1995, he sparkled in the World Series (2–0, 1.29) and was named its MVP.

64 A. In his playing days he was a catalyst who did what only a few men have done: He won back-to-back MVPs.

B. He packed a lot of punch into his 5-foot-7, 160-pound frame, and helped the Reds win five division titles between the years 1972 and 1979. They also won the World Series with him as their second baseman in 1975 and 1976.

C. He was a rather unusual number-three hitter (although he did hit in other spots in the order over his career), given the position he played and his size, but in 1976, he became the fifth second sacker to drive in 100+ in a season, and his single-season home-run high was 27.

65 A. This intimidating pitcher's nickname was "The Barber" because he ceaselessly threw up and in on batters, giving them a very close shave, and without the benefit of lather.

B. He was the losing pitcher when Don Larsen threw his World Series perfect game in 1956, and, coincidentally, had been the last man prior to Larsen to come up with a no-hitter, just 13 days before Larsen's gem. He was also the Giants' starting pitcher the day Bobby Thomson hit his "shot heard 'round the world" to win the 1951 NL flag.

C. He completed a rare trifecta, playing for three teams in New York: the Giants, Dodgers, and Yankees.

66 A. He was the first reliever to hit the 40-save level in a season (45 in 1983).

B. A submarine-style pitcher, he induced many a harmless grounder. This Royals star was also stingy in giving up walks, exhibiting pinpoint control.

C. "Quiz" was famous for his colorful quotes, such as, "I've seen the future and it's much like the present, only longer."

67 A. In 1992, this outfielder (1973–95) became the oldest man to reach the century mark for RBIs in a season.

B. A seven-time Gold Glover, he is most remembered for his days with the Padres and Yankees.

C. This Hall of Famer is also recalled for being drafted by the NFL, NBA, ABA, and for the time he, after completing his between-innings warm-up throws, threw a ball to the batboy, but instead of reaching its destination, the ball struck and killed a seagull in Toronto.

68 A. In 2004 this lefty became, at almost 41 years of age, the oldest pitcher to craft a perfect game.

B. He's a five-time Cy Young winner, second most ever, who has led his league in Ks on nine occasions. He shared the MVP Award in the 2001 World Series when his D-backs knocked off the Yankees.

C. His 10.61 batters fanned per nine innings once ranked number one all-time (it's #3 through 2019). One of his fastballs actually hit a bird in flight, virtually atomizing it.

69 A. In 2006, this man led the NL in homers and RBIs (a feat he duplicated in 2008), and became just the second player to win both the MVP and the Rookie of the Year Award in consecutive seasons.

B. His 58 HR and 149 RBIs in 2006 were the highest totals ever for a "sophomore." He followed up with 47 (second in the league), then 48 homers (again tops in the NL) then 45 over the next three seasons.

C. This Phillies muscleman also won the 2006 All-Star Game Home Run Derby.

70 A. His 2006 victory total, 16, was the lowest for a starting pitcher who had won the Cy Young Award during a full season—that has since changed drastically with Jacob deGrom winning

the award with a 10–9 record in 2018. In addition, his lifetime mark at the end of '06 was only two games above .500.

B. He was also the first NL hurler to earn the Cy Young and have an ERA above 3.00 since Steve Carlton did this in 1982. He led all pitchers in ground ball-out ratio in 2005 and 2006.

C. The D-backs star's 2006 victory total did lead the league, though, and his ERA of 3.10 ranked third. In 2007 he won 18 before going 22–7 in 2008, once more leading the NL in victories. He would appear in just one more big league game.

71 A. A member of the Red Sox from 2006 through his 2010 retirement, this man still ranks high for many Marlins power categories, from lifetime homers to runs driven in.

B. A fine third baseman, he won a Gold Glove in 2005.

C. On average, he was normally good for around 20+ HR and 90 or so RBIs per year.

72 A. No Arizona center fielder ever hit more homers than this man's 35 in 2000. In 2004, he departed the Diamondbacks and later played for the Dodgers, Angels, Giants, and Rockies.

B. He was also a five-time Gold Glove winner, and was one of only eight men to rap 300+ homers and swipe 300 or more bases. Additionally, only he and Mays had 425+ doubles and 100 or more triples to go along with the 300+ home runs and stolen bases.

C. In 2006, when he was 41, this man became the first player over 40 to bang out more than eight triples since Honus Wagner did it way back in 1915.

73 A. This outfielder is also in the 300 HR/300 SB club (with over 300 doubles as well). In 2005, when he established a new NLDS record with his 10 RBIs with the Cardinals, he was appearing in his fifth postseason over the past six years.

B. From 1998 through 2006 he played for eight different clubs.

C. His initials are "R.S."

74 A. A menacing figure at the plate, this powerful lefty propelled 475 homers. He is one of only a few men to hoist homers over the right-field roof at Forbes Field.

B. He would twirl his bat with an exaggerated windmill motion prior to every pitch.

C. "Pops" was team captain of the "We Are Family" Pittsburgh Pirates, and, in 1979, shared the MVP with Keith Hernandez in the first-ever tie for that honor.

75 A. On three occasions this righty won 25+ games and did not win the Cy Young Award.

B. A Hall of Famer, he had more deliveries than UPS, and his high leg kick made his windup unique.

C. He is often remembered for the time he hit John Roseboro over the head with a bat, but he should also be recalled for his 243 wins and sizzling .631 won-loss percentage.

○ ○ ○ **2** ○ ○ ○

ANSWERS

1 Eddie Mathews

2 Roger Maris, who hit only 275 lifetime blasts. Although his next-highest season home-run output was a rather meager 39 (in 1960), and although after 1962, when he hit 33 homers, he never hit more than 26 home runs in a season, he did hold the coveted single-season home-run record until Mark McGwire came along to shatter it with 70 HR in 1998.

3 Willie McCovey

4 Ernie Banks

5 Kenny Lofton. His nomadic ways really picked up around the turn of the century as he spent 2001 with Cleveland, split 2002 with the White Sox and Giants, played for both the Pirates and Cubs in 2003, was a Yankee in 2004, a Philly the next year, was with the Dodgers in 2006, and spent time with Texas and Cleveland in 2007. Incidentally, in college he was the sixth man for the Arizona Wildcats team that made it to the Final Four in 1988. The only other big leaguer to appear in a Final Four and a World Series was pitcher Tim Stoddard. Coincidentally, both those men attended the same high school.

6 Rickey Henderson. He is also the all-time leader for home runs hit by a leadoff hitter and for runs scored. Plus, only Barry Bonds has drawn more walks than Henderson. This all-time great was unusual in that he threw left-handed but hit righty. Trivia item: On April 24, 1987, Phil Niekro and Steve Carlton worked a game for Cleveland and Henderson homered off both, marking the only time a batter has connected against two 300-game winners in a game.

7 Eddie Murray, a high school teammate of Ozzie Smith's at Locke High School in Los Angeles.

8 Cal Ripken Jr. He's still best remembered for his incredible record streak of playing in 2,632 games. Through 2019, only Mariano Rivera, with 100 percent of the votes, Ken Griffey at 99.32 percent, Tom Seaver, with 98.84 percent, and Nolan Ryan, at 98.79 percent, pulled down a higher percentage of votes than Ripken did. One member of the media who did not cast one of his ten votes (the maximum permitted) for Ripken explained that he didn't feel Ripken needed his vote, saying he wanted to lend his support to ten other players instead. Had every voter felt that way, Ripken would have been denied Hall of Fame status in 2007. It would certainly seem that a voter's job is simply to cast a YES vote if a player is undeniably deserving of the honor, and not think beyond that.

9 Roberto Clemente. Only five men ever won more Gold Gloves than Clemente. He will also be forever remembered for his tragic death on New Year's Eve in 1972; while on a mercy mission to deliver relief supplies to earthquake victims in Nicaragua, his plane crashed at sea. His body was never recovered.

10 Tony Gwynn. After his initial season, 1982, he surpassed the .300 plateau every single season of his career through 2001, when he hit .324 at the age of 41. He even seriously flirted with the .400 level in 1994 when he wound up hitting .394. He is, along with Ty Cobb and Ted Williams, one of three men to win two batting crowns with averages *below* their lifetime marks.

11 Derek Jeter

12 Robin Yount. His brother, Larry, made it to the majors for one game but was hurt during his warm-up throws and never faced a single batter in the bigs.

13 Mel Ott. This left-handed hitter's odd batting stance featured him drastically raising his right leg prior to meeting the ball. In 1943, Ott drew a record-tying seven consecutive walks over a three-day period, and, in late 1929, coaxed a then-record six walks in a doubleheader when the Phillies worked him carefully to help Philadelphia's Chuck Klein secure the home-run crown. (One source has all five of his walks in the second game as being intentional ones.) Klein wound up with 43 homers to Ott's 42.

14 Jason Varitek

15 Trot Nixon

16 Livan Hernandez. His half brother Orlando, also known as "El Duque," defected several years after his brother did. Orlando did so with seven others on the day after Christmas in 1997, and was rescued by the Bahamian Coast Guard three days after landing on a Caribbean island.

17 Joe Carter

18 Gary Carter. As a seven-year-old, he was the "Punt, Pass, and Kick Contest" national champ in 1961, the first year that competition was held.

19 Roberto Alomar. Trivia items: His first big league hit came in 1988 versus fireballing Nolan Ryan. Three years later, when the "Ryan Express" engineered his record seventh no-hitter, Alomar made the final out. Furthermore, when Ryan notched his first two no-hitters, the second baseman behind him was Sandy Alomar Sr. Incidentally, Ryan lost five additional no-hitters in the ninth innings of those games.

20 Jason Bay. His hometown of Trail also produced another Rookie of the Year—NHL's Barret Jackman, a former St. Louis Blues defenseman.

21 Harmon Killebrew

22 Mike Piazza. Interestingly, this amazing stick got a chance in the majors due to fortuitous circumstances rather than based on sheer talent. His father Vince was a childhood acquaintance of longtime Dodgers coach and manager, Tommy Lasorda, both having grown up in Norristown, Pennsylvania. Lasorda is, in fact, the godfather of one of Mike's brothers. So, as a favor to Vince, Lasorda drafted Mike, but not until the 62nd round of the 1988 draft, making Mike the very last selection that year. One could easily argue that it also made him the greatest late, late pick ever. As an added trivia note, when Mike was 12 years old, he took hitting lessons from Ted Williams in a batting cage set up in Piazza's backyard.

23 Warren Spahn. Of all the major leaguers who served in the military, only "Spahnie," of "Spahn and [Johnny] Sain and pray for rain" fame, earned a battlefield commission. He was the oldest pitcher ever to win 20 games and the only one to win ERA crowns in three decades. Additionally, no pitcher ever led his league in wins more times than this artist (eight times in all).

24 Mark McGwire. For the record, and by way of comparison, a stunning 68.6 percent of Bonds' hits in 2001 were for extra bases, including, of course, his 73 home runs.

25 Mike Schmidt

26 Ichiro Suzuki. Oddity: After getting permission from the American League, he has his first—but not his last—name on the back of his jersey.

27 Craig Biggio

28 Hank Aaron

29 Moises Alou. The game in which Bartman got in Alou's way was played exactly 95 years after the Cubs had last nailed down a world championship. And yet another trivia note, Moises is not only the son of Felipe and the nephew of Matty and Jesus, but he is also the cousin of pitcher Mel Rojas, who, like Moises, once played under Felipe in Montreal.

30 Mark Prior

31 Lou Brock

32 Bill Freehan. In college, at the University of Michigan where he also played football, he set a Big Ten all-time record when he hit a celestial .585 in 1961. Upon his retirement, his lifetime fielding average was .993, then the best ever.

33 Rogers Hornsby. While his first name is very unusual, another ballplayer with that first name (pitcher Rogers Hornsby McKee), no doubt named after the great hitter, did make it to the majors. He was no Hornsby, lasting just five games during two World War II seasons—1943, when he made his debut as a 16 year old and 1944 (5.87 lifetime ERA, with a 1–0 slate).

34 Barry Larkin. The game in which his brother was inserted into the Reds lineup as the first baseman, by request of Barry (he told team officials that he had always wanted to play on the same big league diamond with his younger brother), was the only game Stephen Larkin would ever play in the majors. He went 1-for-3, meaning he could boast that he had a better lifetime batting average than Barry's .295.

35 Kenny Rogers

36 Grover Cleveland Alexander

37 Carlton Fisk. His memorable World Series moment was, of course, the home run he hit down the left-field line in Fenway off Cincinnati's Pat Darcy—the one which he "willed" to stay fair by gesturing with his arms. The ball bounced off the foul pole, and that homer forced a seventh game of that classic World Series of '75. He is also one of just two modern-day catchers to have led his league in triples; the other one was Tim McCarver.

38 Michael Young

39 Willie Wilson. Trivia: In the 1980 World Series, Wilson set a negative record when he fanned 12 times in 26 at bats, with his final strikeout ignominiously ending the Series.

40 Bob Gibson

69

NAME THAT BALLPLAYER

41 Denny McLain. He is the only 30-game winner who went on to drop 20 decisions, and he did that when he went 10–22 just three years after his greatest success.

42 Andy Pettitte

43 Billy Williams

44 CC Sabathia

45 Dontrelle Willis

46 Jose Canseco. According to Baseball Almanac's website, the Cansecos are one of ten sets of twins to make it to the majors.

47 Omar Vizquel

48 Tug McGraw

49 Hank Greenberg. Between Babe Ruth in 1927 and Roger Maris in 1961, no man hit more than Greenberg's 58 HR in 1938. In 1935, when he wound up with 170 RBIs, he drove in exactly 100 runs by the All-Star break. Remarkably, he did not make the AL squad.

50 Fergie Jenkins. He was such a fine athlete that he, like Bob Gibson, played basketball for the Harlem Globetrotters.

51 Todd Helton. He played baseball and football at the University of Tennessee and was, in fact, the second-string quarterback—behind Jerry Colquitt—in his junior year. When Colquitt went down with an injury, Helton was the starter, but soon, due to an injury he sustained, Helton lost his job to Peyton Manning, who went on to establish many school records before going on to NFL greatness.

52 Steve Garvey

53 Christy Mathewson. It took him just 12 full seasons to reach the 300-win mark, an all-time record.

54 Fred Lynn

55 Roy Halladay

56 Don Mattingly

57 Don Drysdale. Because he was such a brushback artist, Orlando Cepeda observed: "The trick against Drysdale is to hit him before he hits you."

58 Al Kaline

59 Bo Jackson

60 Alfonso Soriano

61 Don Newcombe

62 David Wright

63 Tom Glavine

64 Joe Morgan

65 Sal Maglie

66 Dan Quisenberry

67 Dave Winfield

68 Randy Johnson

69 Ryan Howard. The first man who won the MVP the year after being named the Rookie of the Year was Cal Ripken Jr. Meanwhile, two men—Fred Lynn and Ichiro Suzuki—won both of those awards in the same season.

70 Brandon Webb

71 Mike Lowell

72 Steve Finley

73 Reggie Sanders

74 Willie Stargell

75 Juan Marichal

○ ○ ○ **3** ○ ○ ○

THE MIDDLE INNINGS

1 A. Not until Johnny Bench came along did most experts change their opinion on which player was the greatest catcher ever. The player in question here had been, almost universally, accepted as *the* best. This Yankee wore a single-digit uniform number.

   B. In fact, he shared his #8 with Yogi Berra, an oddity in that both men are listed as having that jersey number retired by the same team.

   C. This all-time great had the initials "B.D."

2 A. In 1967 this man carried his club to the American League pennant by hitting .523 over the last 12 games with five homers and 16 RBIs. His team required a sweep of a season-ending series in order to prevent a three-way tie with the Detroit Tigers and the Minnesota Twins, and this man, a proverbial one-man wrecking crew, went 7-for-8 with five runs driven in.

   B. He is better known by his three-letter nickname than by his difficult-to-spell alphabet soup of a last name.

   C. He won the Most Valuable Player award and a Triple Crown in the 1967 season, known to Red Sox fans as "The Impossible Dream" year. In the meantime, his .301 average in 1968 represents the lowest average that was good enough to win a batting crown.

3 A. In late 2006, this often-overlooked outfielder signed a $126 million contract (a seven-year extension), tied then for the sixth-largest overall deal in baseball annals.

B. He blossomed in 2002, his first of three 100-RBI campaigns, then hit a career-high .317 the following season. By 2004 he had won the first of three straight Gold Glove Awards for his excellence in center field.

C. His Blue Jays fully realized that they had to hold on to this nucleus of their squad after he hit .303 with 106 RBIs and made the All-Star team in 2006. Although he sagged to .245 in 2007, he bounced back to hit .300 in 2008.

4 A. The first name this man went by is, literally, a spice, although his nickname, "The Wild Horse of the Osage," addressed his berserk style of play. He had equine speed, leading his league in stolen bases three times.

B. He was a rugged, colorful member of the St. Louis Cardinals crew known as "The Gashouse Gang," and this outfielder/ third baseman hit a ton in World Series play. His .418 life-time batting average in Series play ranked fourth best all-time, even decades later as baseball entered the 21st century.

C. He also played professional football for a short time, but, as a four-time All-Star and a .298 lifetime hitter, was obviously a better baseball player.

5 A. This man, with the unusual middle name of Morning, was a blur on the basepaths. He was also a member of a Los Angeles Dodgers infield completely made up of switch-hitters.

B. He became the first speed merchant to top the 100-stolen-base barrier when he burgled 104 bases in 1962, eclipsing the old mark (96 in 1915) held by Ty Cobb. He won the MVP that season while hitting only .299.

C. His son, also a big leaguer, may not have stolen as many bases as his father, but he was hardly a "speed bump," stealing 196 bags over six seasons.

6 A. This man was the possessor of perhaps the nastiest slider ever. He fanned 4,136 batters, making him, until rather recently, the all-time strikeout king for southpaws.

B. He was infamous for his feud with the media, and probably the first true superstar to declare a vow of silence with the press.

C. He was so dominant that his peers began to identify him as "Lefty." Considering how many great southpaws the game has seen, it's quite a compliment that when someone simply mentioned "Lefty," everybody immediately knew who was being discussed. He was, after all, the man who went 27–10, good for a .730 won-loss percentage, in 1972 when his team, the Phillies, finished sixth in the six-team National League East Division with a miserable 59–97 record. He thereby accounted for nearly half of the Phillies wins that year (45.76 percent, to be exact).

7 A. This third baseman (he also played some first base), who attended Arizona State University, is one of a handful of men to swat four home runs in a single game.

B. His final season, 1988, was spent with the Cardinals, but the rest of his career found him in an Atlanta Braves uniform.

C. In 1978 he won the Rookie of the Year Award.

8 A. This AL infielder from the Eastern Division played from 2001 through 2014, getting his first taste of real recognition in 2004 when he lashed out 50 doubles to lead the league.

B. The following season he came back with an additional 45 two-baggers, hit .314 (fifth best in the league), and made the All-Star team. In 2008 he crushed 51 doubles then improved to 56, a personal high which led the AL.

C. This Baltimore star, a native of Durham, North Carolina, attended college at both the University of South Carolina and the University of North Carolina.

9 A. This player, who played from 1997 through 2008, was mainly a second baseman. He played his first ten seasons with the same NL team, albeit in two different cities due to a shift of his franchise in 2005.

B. He hit .300 from 1999 through 2003 and was a lifetime .298 hitter.

C. The Puerto Rico native was an All-Star in 2000 when he hit a career-high .330, and again in 2002 and 2003, the year he won a Silver Slugger Award.

10 A. This outfielder's career ran 19 years with the A's, Cubs, and Dodgers, ending in 1984. His most productive season resulted in 32 HR, his only 30-plus-home-run season, and 77 RBIs, but that year, 1976, he gained recognition for something beyond his baseball stats.

B. His biggest fame came on April 25 in America's bicentennial year. He was stationed in the outfield for the Cubs in a game at Los Angeles when two protesters dashed onto the playing surface, placed an American flag on the field, doused it with lighter fluid, and then attempted to set it on fire. The player in question dashed over and rescued the flag. Moments later the Dodger Stadium scoreboard flashed the message, _____ (the name of the player), YOU MADE A GREAT PLAY.

C. Big clue: His last name is the same as a day of the week.

11 A. This man played primarily for the Montreal Expos, where he won the 1977 Rookie of the Year Award, and for the Chicago Cubs, where he earned the 1987 MVP Award.

B. In 1987, the strong-armed outfielder racked up 12 assists, a fine total, albeit shy of his personal high of 17 in 1978, and had offensive stats so marvelous—137 RBIs and 49 home runs (when 49 homers *really* meant something)—he won the MVP with a last-place club, an unheard-of accomplishment.

C. For quite some time some of his teammates such as Ryne Sandberg lobbied to have this player inducted into the Hall of Fame, but it took until 2010 for the man known as "The Hawk" to gain entrance in Cooperstown.

12 A. This pitcher won 31 games (versus a mere four losses) in 1930 and was his league's MVP, a rare feat for a pitcher, the following year. In fact, he won the pitchers' version of the Triple

Crown in both of those seasons, leading the AL in strikeouts, ERA, and wins.

B. He also led his league in strikeouts seven times in a row, from 1925 through 1931, and was the ERA leader for *nine* seasons, a positively magnificent record which still stands. He ended his career with exactly 300 wins and a .680 won-loss percentage.

C. He was discovered by Jack Dunn, the same man who signed Babe Ruth to his first contract. Dunn later sold the pitcher in question to the Philadelphia A's for $100,600, at the time, the largest-ever sale of a player. Oddity: He is also one of two men who gave up a homer to Ruth during his record-setting 1927 season, and a hit to Joe DiMaggio during his 1941 record-setting 56-game hitting streak.

13 A. This player's father was a successful wide receiver (once named to the Pro Bowl game) in the NFL, from 1965 to 1975, with the Los Angeles Rams. He came off the Notre Dame campus where he had been an All-American.

B. The player in question was a smooth-fielding first baseman— he won six consecutive Gold Glove Awards, from 1995 through 2000—and is most associated with the Giants, where he joined the broadcasting team for the 2007 season, thus following in his father's footsteps; his dad, Jack, had also broadcast games (for the Rams, before his death in 2006).

C. In the fifth game of the 2002 World Series, this player scored on a Kenny Lofton triple and made a different type of defensive play: He swooped up three-year-old Darren Baker (son of Giants manager Dusty), who was serving as the batboy that day. Darren had run into the home-plate vicinity—and thus into harm's way—to retrieve Lofton's bat.

14. A. A utility player with a zany sense of humor, this man played from 1987 to 1998 for the Orioles, Rangers, Indians, and Tigers. In Baltimore he played under his father, who coached and managed there for years.

B. One moment of infamy came when his 1989 Fleer baseball card revealed an obscenity scrawled on the knob of his bat.

C. Most of his play came at second base, where he, on occasion with the Orioles, teamed up to turn double plays with his more-famous brother.

15 A. This obscure player, who made his major league debut on September 1, 2005, with the Orioles, is reportedly, at more than 320 pounds (listed at 322, to be precise), the heaviest player ever to don a big league uniform.

B. After turning down a chance to play football at Louisiana State University, the 6-foot-5 first baseman/designated hitter signed with the Pirates organization. His initials are "W.Y."

C. He later spent a short time with the Padres and Astros organizations. His power, some scouts believed, might enable him to stick in the majors someday; in 2005, although in batting practice and not in a game, he smashed a ball that reached the B & O Warehouse beyond the right-field wall at Camden Yards in Baltimore. However, his only stint in the bigs was a brief 14 games in 2005 for the O's.

16 A. A fine reliever from 1969 through 1988, this righty was one of the best sidearm pitchers ever.

B. On August 1, 1978, he retired Pete Rose to snap a 44-game hitting streak. After the game Rose was livid, saying the pitcher got him out on soft stuff instead of challenging him. The reliever, defending his style, replied, "He gets paid to get hits. I get paid to get outs."

C. He ranked first on the Atlanta Braves all-time save list until John Smoltz came along to shoot by him.

17 A. This man experienced several seasons of greatness, but was not, by the Hall of Fame yardstick, great, coming up just shy of such a lofty status. Still, he swatted 398 homers, joined the 30-home run/30-stolen base club back when hitting 30+ homers was still noteworthy, and is one of a handful of men to win back-to-back MVP Awards.

B. He broke in as a catcher, but many of his throws wound up not in the glove of a second baseman or shortstop, but in center field instead—the position he'd convert to and where he'd go on to win five Gold Glove Awards.

C. A devout Mormon, he was a true good guy of the game with a spotless reputation, winning both the Lou Gehrig Memorial Award (1985) and the Roberto Clemente Award (1988). All but 27 of his home runs came while he was in an Atlanta uniform, a big reason the Braves retired his #3 jersey in 1994.

18 A. Like the man mentioned above, this player, a second-sacker (1981–94), had difficulties with routine throws; many felt he had a mental block when it came to such plays.

B. Teammate Pedro Guerrero, also a shaky defensive infielder, was asked what went through his mind when his team was on defense in tight spots. He, only half-jokingly, replied, "First, I pray to God that nobody hits the ball to me. Then, I pray to God nobody hits the ball to _____."

C. To be fair, the man in question was a five-time All-Star, was one of a slew of Dodgers to win the Rookie of the Year Award (1982), and was a solid .281 lifetime hitter.

19 A. This rather diminutive lefty (listed at 5-foot-10 and 180 pounds) was one of the greatest relievers ever.

B. In 2006 his 40 saves marked the second time he had reached that level (his best was 44 with Houston in 2003, and he accumulated between 37 and 39 on four other occasions). He attended Ferrum College (Virginia) and set season NCAA records for the highest strikeouts per nine innings pitched, a simply sensational 19.1 in 1992, and for the fewest hits allowed per nine innings (1.58). Further, his 327 Ks over 182 ⅓ innings established a Division III record for career strikeouts.

C. Even though it's hard to fathom, this player originally threw righty; but after twice breaking that arm, he taught himself to throw southpaw. He concluded his career with 422 saves, sixth best all-time through the 2019 season.

20 A. In 2006 this man became just the eighth NL hurler since 1960 to lead his league in wins, with 16, and strikeouts (216). His 35 starts and six complete games also led all NL pitchers.

B. Although not a huge name, the 6-foot-7 righty was clearly the ace of the Reds staff, even though his previous two seasons with Cincinnati produced modest 10–9 and 11–13 pitching slates. Since his big year in 2006, he put up a 16–6 season before agonizing through a 6–17 year in 2008 when, this time, he led his league in losses.

C. He actually began his big league days with Oakland in 2002, after being drafted by the Rangers three years earlier. Big clue: his first name is the same as the last name of the man many people still consider to be the true all-time home run champion.

21 A. This outfielder/designated hitter began his career with the Red Sox in 1987, and finished back there for a short stint (11 games) in 2004, with pit stops in between in Chicago with the White Sox, in San Francisco, and in Cleveland. He had his finest years as a member of the Colorado Rockies, exploiting the thin air there, a boon for hitters.

B. In 1996, this man, Vinny Castilla (40), and Andres Galarraga (47) became the second trio of teammates in baseball history to all contribute 40 or more homers.

C. This player also exploded for a career-high 40 home runs in 1996, with personal highs for average (.344) and runs driven in, with 128. By the way (not that this clue should help much): His middle name is very unusual—it's Rena.

22 A. The first time three teammates each hit 40+ homers came in 1973 when an Atlanta Braves threesome managed this feat. They were Hank Aaron, Dusty Baker, and this man.

B. Like Baker, this man went on to become a successful big league manager, with the New York Mets, Cincinnati, Baltimore, Los Angeles, and Washington (2011–13). As a player, this All-Star and three-time Gold Glover primarily spent time with the O's.

C. His 43 homers in '73 established a single-season high by a second baseman.

23 A. Speaking of power-hitting second basemen, this man, last active in 2008 with the Dodgers, emerged as the most prolific home-run-hitting second-sacker ever, blowing past greats such as Joe Morgan and eventually the reigning king, Ryne Sandberg (in 2004). His lifetime total stands at 377.

B. He won the NL MVP in 2000 when he was with San Francisco.

C. His feud—some called it a clash of egos—with Barry Bonds made big news when both men played for the Giants and glowered at each other across the clubhouse.

24 A. In 1966 this outfielder won the NL batting crown (.342), and of his 183 hits, all but 29 were singles. As a leadoff hitter with very little punch, he realized his job was simply to flick at the ball, use all fields, bunt, and cajole his way on base any way he could.

B. Two of his brothers also played in the majors.

C. In fact, when they were all with the Giants, there was a time when all three of them were in the game at the same time, covering the entire outfield for the G-men. That oddity was unprecedented, and has never since been duplicated. One account indicates that two brothers started the game and the third replaced center fielder Willie Mays in the seventh inning. In the eighth, the three brothers went down in order at the plate.

25 A. "He's not that big in stature," Andre Dawson observed of this first baseman, who ended his career after the 2005 season with 449 homers. "He's compact—very strong. He's got an

uppercut type of swing, and he gets the bat head through the strike zone real quick."

B. After sustaining several injuries, this man, who spent his entire career with the Houston Astros, was one of several stars to wear "armor," in his case protecting his hand.

C. His unorthodox batting stance was most noteworthy for how far apart his legs were spread as he prepared to take his cut and for how he didn't stride forward at all as the pitch came in—yet he still managed to generate a whole lot of power.

26 A. This mighty outfielder was infamous for his volatility; his ongoing battles with the media were legendary, and he even had several run-ins with the law after he retired at the end of 2000.

B. If a pitcher brushed him back or hit him, or if an opposing manager accused him of corking his bat, as Boston manager Kevin Kennedy once did, this strongman became as incensed as he was intent.

C. He instilled fear in pitchers with the same gut-wrenching emotional punch of a Don Vito Corleone can't-refuse offer. He was, in fact, the first man to hit 50 or more doubles and 50+ homers in a single season.

27 A. Ken Griffey Jr. and this man once shared the record for having hit at least one home run in the most big league parks—43.

B. His nickname, "Crime Dog," tied in (as a play on words) with his last name. This man is the cousin of catcher Charles Johnson, and his brother Terry also made it to the bigs.

C. The lefty with the big power cut—some likened it to the snap of a buggy whip—wound up his playing days tied with Lou Gehrig for the 21st spot on the all-time home-run list, with 493.

28 A. A southpaw, this man surrendered Roberto Clemente's 3,000th (and final) big league hit in 1972.

B. With the Mets from his rookie year of 1971 through 1977, he was part of a fine pitching staff that included Tom Seaver and Jerry Koosman.

C. Over his 13 years spent entirely with the Mets and Texas, his career record was one game below .500 (125–126), although most experts felt he was a fine pitcher and his stats support that contention. He fanned 1,516 men (more than double his walk total), he gave up fewer hits than innings pitched, and his ERA sparkled at 3.18 lifetime.

29 A. Ellis Burks, a former teammate of this man, asserted that the star outfielder had "always been a good hitter, but you put him in a great situation like [in] Coors Field, it's just going to enhance his ability." Burks was correct. The man in question hit well in Montreal, where he broke in, but all five of his 100+ RBI seasons came with the Rockies.

B. This player was a winner of seven Gold Gloves, but is often remembered for an amusing gaffe: Thinking a catch he had made resulted in the third out of an inning, he handed the ball to a young fan sitting in the stands.

C. Another anecdote involving this one-time MVP took place in the 1997 All-Star game. A pitch from Randy Johnson vapor-trailed its way several feet from this man's head; before the next pitch, he turned his batting helmet around and stepped to the other side of the plate, wanting no part of a lefty-on-lefty confrontation with Johnson.

30 A. During his early days in San Francisco, this promising young-ster roamed the same San Francisco outfield with Willie Mays, prompting inevitable comparisons and claims that he would evolve into "the next Willie Mays." An often-shown highlight clip features a superb Mays catch taking place while colliding with this man.

B. He played from 1968 through 1981 with eight different clubs, being involved in six trades—the first being to the Yankees from the Giants for Bobby Murcer.

C. The father of an all-time great, this man is, like his son, a mem-ber of the "30/30 Club," having hit 30 or more homers while stealing 30+ bases in the same season on several occasions.

31 A. In the batter's box, this man was as jittery as a double-shot espresso addict.

B. Younger baseball fans probably know this man best for his managerial days, especially his successful tenure with the Indians during their glory days (circa 1994–99).

C. His antics, and especially the length of time it took him to get set at the plate, earned him the nickname "The Human Rain Delay," but don't be fooled; this man could hit. He won the 1974 Rookie of the Year Award, hit .290 lifetime, and was an AL All-Star in 1975 as a member of the Texas Rangers.

32 A. During the 1934 World Series, this Cardinals star slid hard into the Tigers third baseman, infuriating the Detroit throng. Later, when he took his position in the outfield, fans rained down a shower of fruit and garbage on him. After the game he wryly commented, "I know why they threw it at me. What I can't figure out is why they brought it to the ballpark in the first place."

B. He went on to win the Triple Crown and the NL MVP in 1937, and was inducted into the Hall of Fame in 1968.

C. The .324 lifetime hitter often went by "Ducky."

33 A. The most pivotal play in the 1986 World Series involved this man, a member of the New York Mets at the time.

B. He is also the stepfather of outfielder Preston Wilson.

C. His real name is William, but nobody calls him that. Final clue: He played his entire career, a dozen seasons, with the Mets and the Blue Jays.

34 A. He spent 1997 through 2002 with the Twins, and then gained greater acclaim with Boston, coming up big in many key situations for the Red Sox. He even won the MVP of the classic 2004 ALCS and the World Series MVP in 2013 when he hit .688.

B. The 2004 postseason in general was huge for this big man with a big stick. He hit an utterly fantastic .545 in the division series versus Anaheim, .387 with three home runs in the next round against the Yankees, and then .308 in the World Series versus the Cardinals. In the 2007 ALDS he hit .714, going 5-for-7.

C. In 2006 he ripped a career-high 54 home runs, 10 more than his nearest competitor. However, his next two seasons produced only 58 additional homers. Nevertheless, when he retired after the 2016 season, he owned 541 home runs and 632 doubles, #12 all-time.

35 A. His 288 lifetime wins, which was the seventh-highest total by a lefty, has somehow not been enough to get this star into the Hall of Fame; he is the winningest pitcher *not* honored in the Hall. He won 20 games with the Dodgers once, and twice with the Yankees.

B. He endured forever in the majors, spending 26 seasons there, longer than any pitcher save Nolan Ryan, quitting at the age of 46. He was traded three times—once in a three-team swap, and once for Dick Allen.

C. While Lou Gehrig had a disease named after him, this man had a revolutionary surgical procedure, an arm operation, named in his honor when he took part in medical history, receiving a "bionic" arm in 1974. He would go on to win 164 games after surgery.

36 A. While Roberto and Sandy Alomar are the only brothers to win the MVP in an All-Star game, this man and his son are the only father-son combo to win that trophy.

B. A vital cog in the "Big Red Machine," this man held down the job for Cincinnati in right field.

C. He and his son, in more ways than one, made history when they became teammates in Seattle.

37 A. As was the case with the man in the previous question, this player, a Gold Glove infielder, was also a part of the "Big Red Machine."

B. In fact, along with Tony Perez, Joe Morgan, George Foster, and the man from the last question, this player made up the five

"Big Red" players who won an All-Star MVP Award from 1967 through 1982.

C. Still a legend in his home country of Venezuela, he became the prototype and idol for future big league shortstops from that nation, such as Omar Vizquel.

38 A. The 2006 season was called this player's breakthrough year, as he led the majors in runs, extra base hits, and topped the AL in doubles.

B. Some would argue that 2005, when he was just 22 years old, was actually his "I have arrived" year, as he took over the starting center-field job from Coco Crisp and scored 111 runs in his first full season.

C. His 53 two-base hits in '05 represented the third-highest total in Cleveland Indians history. Further, his 90 RBIs in 2008 was a personal high, and a fine total for a man who hit leadoff almost all the time.

39 A. This strongman retired with 612 home runs (#8 lifetime), which helped him gain Hall of Fame status.

B. With the Phillies he led the NL in homers in 2003—the only time he achieved that feat—but he began his career in the Junior Circuit where he returned in 2006 with the White Sox. He later bounced around to the Dodgers, Twins, and back to his original club, the Indians. He finished off his 22-year career in 2012, splitting time between the Phillies and Orioles.

C. His strikeout totals each year were enormous—with highs of 185 and 182—and he reached 100 strikeouts in every full season he played from 1995 to 2004. However, somewhat contradictorily, he had a good eye, he was a respected hitter (.276 lifetime), and he drew tons of walks, too—normally between 100 and 120 or so in his prime. Toss in the fact that he finished first, second, or third in his leagues for the most walks drawn eight times.

40 A. In college he was a punter for the University of Nebraska, was a part of the Cornhuskers national championship squad of

1994, and coached that university's baseball team from 2012 to 2019.

B. Prior to 2007, he had been with the Angels ever since he first broke in to the big leagues in 1996. He has won a Gold Glove as both an outfielder and a first baseman.

C. In 2000, he was so hot he reached the 100-hit plateau quicker—in just 61 games—than any player since Heinie Manush achieved that feat in 60 games. For real trivia buffs, he caught the final out in Game 7 of the 2002 World Series.

41 A. When Willie Stargell covered left field in 1974, this man was establishing himself as the team's second baseman.

B. His highest batting average came in 1977 when he hit .336 over 453 at bats, good enough to finish immediately behind teammate Dave Parker, the batting champ that year, if, that is, he had had enough at bats to qualify for the league leadership.

C. It was on September 16, 1975, though, that this contact hitter turned in a sterling 7-for-7 performance at Wrigley Field, making him the only modern-day player to collect seven hits during a nine-inning contest. That day his Pirates pounded the Cubs, 22–0, good for the largest shutout in the modern era. The following day this player slashed out three more hits for a record ten over a two-game span.

42 A. He began his career in 1975 with the Giants and went on to jack 340 home runs, mainly as a right fielder.

B. He hit .381 in the 1985 NLCS, was in the top ten for homers seven times (usually good for around 25 to 30 HR when healthy), and led the NL in slugging once.

C. Probably his most famous feat was his ninth-inning homer versus Dodgers pitcher Tom Niedenfuer on October 16, 1985, ensuring that the Cardinals won the NL flag. Los Angeles fans still cannot believe that, with first base open and an intentional walk in order, Dodgers skipper Tommy Lasorda ordered Niedenfuer to throw to this man.

43 A. When he was voted into the Hall of Fame in 2001, despite his meager .260 lifetime batting average, there was a maelstrom of controversy. Some ripped the Veterans Committee for voting this man into baseball's pantheon and accused the group of cronyism.

B. Still, he was one of the greatest fielders ever—if not *the* greatest—to cover the right side of the infield. Some experts go beyond that, stating he was the greatest defensive player ever, regardless of position played.

C. Nearly half a century ago he blasted what was the only home run to ever win the World Series in the last half of the ninth inning—the ultimate walk-off homer to be sure.

44 A. When this player was an eight year old, he attended a 1954 doubleheader in St. Louis and witnessed Stan Musial amass five home runs. In 1972, as a member of the San Diego Padres, he smoked five himself during a twin bill versus the Braves. His Padres scored 20 times over the two games; he drove in a record 13 of those runs to break Musial's old mark of 11.

B. Although he was signed originally by the Cardinals and first appeared in the majors with Houston, it was as a charter member of the expansion Padres that he emerged as a star. In his second season with San Diego he punched out 38 homers, and he was an All-Star the following three years.

C. His first name is the same as an all-time NBA great with the last name of Thurmond.

45 A. When John Elway was selected as the 52nd player overall in baseball's 1981 draft, this pitcher went ninth, coming off the Yale campus.

B. To play the name game for clues once more, his last name is a term of endearment, but on the mound this man showed no mercy. From 1983 through 1995, he won 136 contests, winning in double digits six times for the Mets.

C. Like Sid Fernandez, a former teammate who wore #50 as a tribute to the state where he was born, this pitcher was born in Honolulu, Hawaii, the USA's 50th state.

46 A. What a graceful and talented center fielder this man was. First active in 1998, through 2009 he won a Gold Glove Award every season from 2001 on in AL play.

B. In the 2002 All-Star game he made yet another of his patented rob-a-homer catches when he snagged a Barry Bonds drive in right-center. After the game, Sammy Sosa labeled this acrobatic outfielder "Spiderman."

C. Playing for Minnesota all of his career until 2008, he enjoyed several big series in postseason play, reaching an apex of .429 versus the Yankees in the 2003 ALDS.

47 A. Although his bat did contain a great deal of punch—his season high was 33 home runs in 1986—his strikeout totals were alarming. In 1987 he fanned 186 times; only Bobby Bonds had ever gone down on strikes more times in a season. His 186 total still stood as number one on the single-season futility list among AL batters until 2008.

B. He is probably most known for his time spent with the Brewers, where he once led the AL in at bats per home runs. His .220 lifetime batting average set a record for the lowest ever by an outfielder based on 2,000 or more at bats. In addition, his .179 in 1991 when he was with the Tigers represents the lowest batting average ever for a modern outfielder.

C. His last name is the same as a swift animal often the target of hunters.

48 A. This former major leaguer was Michael Jordan's manager in the minors.

B. His playing days, mainly with Montreal, lasted from 1981 to 1990, and in his rookie season a picture appeared in *Sports Illustrated* featuring this man and his father, who also played in the majors, along with Cal Ripken Sr. and Jr., touting the young prospects. If one believes in the *Sports Illustrated* jinx, one could argue that such early exposure plagued the man in question, who recalled, "I ended up getting hurt that year." As a manager, though, he did go on to win the World Series in 2004 and 2007. He also brought a pennant to a pennant-hungry city in 2016.

C. His father Tito nearly won the AL batting title in 1959 when he hit .363 but didn't have enough at bats to qualify for the crown.

49 A. This Phillies outfielder (who later announced their games) hit a fan with a foul ball not once, but twice during an August 17, 1957, contest—and did so on the same at bat! The first ball screeched into the stands and broke Alice Roth's nose. Moments later, as she was being carried away on a stretcher, a foul ball off his bat struck her again.

B. He was inducted into the Hall of Fame in 1995, sporting his lifetime batting average of .308, along with Mike Schmidt. Five times he led the NL in total times reaching base.

C. An oddity: In 1962, as a 35-year-old member of the expansion New York Mets, this man played a position other than the outfield for the first time in his big league days—second base for two games.

50 A. He not only shares the record for the most home runs in a single game with his four back on September 7, 1993, but that day he also tied the record for the most RBIs in a contest, 12, tying the mark set by Jim Bottomley nearly 70 years earlier.

B. Despite such a power outburst, he was never an All-Star, hit only .259 lifetime, and, over 11 seasons managed only an additional 101 home runs beyond his fabulous one-day total.

C. Still, he did earn a nickname which rhymed with his last name. "Hard Hittin'" was his euphonious moniker.

51 A. This long-ball hitter came from a town with the unusual name of Wampum, Pennsylvania.

B. He was the 1964 Rookie of the Year as a Phillie, and won the 1972 AL MVP when he was with the White Sox.

C. Truly an interesting character, at one point in his career, when he was playing first base for the Phillies, he took to "writing" messages of, say, protest (e.g., "Boo," believed to be his response to Philadelphia fans' catcalls) in the dirt with his cleats.

52 A. The 1984 season was an odd one for this pitcher, who spent the first part of the year with the Indians where he languished at 4–5 with a bloated ERA of 5.15. Then, peddled to the Cubs, he was revived, going 16–1, 2.69, then making him one of five pitchers to win 20 while taking the hill for two clubs in a given year.

B. At the tail end of '84, he clinched the pennant-winning game and won the first game of the NLCS versus the Padres, but took the loss in the finale.

C. The 6-foot-7 bearded righty had a colorful nickname right out of military history.

53 A. Like the pitcher in the last question, this man also won 20 games while working for two teams. He began 2002 with the Indians before going to the Expos; he went 10–4 with both clubs. He was traded with Tim Drew to Montreal for four players, including Grady Sizemore.

B. However, it was in 2005 that he emerged at a higher level, going 21–8 for the Angels en route to winning his Cy Young Award.

C. A native of the Dominican Republic, he struggled through 2006 due to a partially torn rotator cuff. He went 1–5 in just 56 ⅓ innings for the Angels and would win just 13 more games over the following three seasons. His revival began in 2013 with Oakland (18–6) and he endured through 2018, quitting at the age of 45.

54 A. What an unbelievable rookie season this man had. In 1997, this shortstop scored 122 times, banged out 209 hits, and reached double figures in homers, triples, and doubles.

B. He made headlines in 2005 when he saved the lives of two women who had fallen into Boston Harbor. In college he was a teammate of Jason Varitek's, and with the Red Sox he was reunited with him.

C. Two additional facts: His first name is his father's first name spelled backwards; he married soccer star Mia Hamm.

55 A. A teammate of Al Kaline, this man hit over .300 just once in his career, in 1961, when he won the batting crown with a whopping .361 average. The next year he hit .243, a record drop of 118 points. He also drove in 132 runs in '61, his career high by far, and some credit his stats that year to his admitted use of corked bats back then. Two years after his pinnacle season he hit for the second-highest average of his 17-year career, a modest .286. He wound up a .271 lifetime hitter.

B. When he retired, only Babe Ruth, Lou Gehrig, and Ted Williams had more AL homers as left-handed hitters than his 377 HR.

C. Only this first baseman and three other men ever won the *Sporting News* Comeback Player of the Year Award twice.

56 A. In 1994 the Giants third baseman was on pace to shatter Roger Maris's single-season home-run record of 61, until a players' strike denied him that opportunity.

B. He won four Gold Glove Awards and hit 378 HR with over 1,200 RBIs before hanging up his cleats in 2003. He made it to the World Series for each of the three teams he played for, winning it all in 2001.

C. He asked to be traded from Cleveland to Arizona in 1997 so he could be closer to his children. His second wife was Michelle Johnson, an actress whose screen debut came in *Blame It on Rio*.

57 A. This man hit a homer in his first big league at-bat on April 23, 1952, and it came off a pitcher who gave up only one career home run (albeit in very few innings pitched). The man in question never again connected over his 21-year career.

B. Mainly a relief pitcher, this Hall of Famer only had 432 at bats, but he won 143 games (with a record 124 of those wins in relief) and saved 227 more.

C. His elusive knuckleball helped him lead the NL in ERA in his rookie season as a reliever (159 ⅓ innings pitched), and again in 1959 when, for the only time in his career, he started more than 11 games. He remains the only reliever to win an ERA crown.

58 A. When this man was traded from the Indians to the Tigers two days before the 1960 season opener, it marked the only time a reigning home-run king was exchanged for the returning batting champ, Harvey Kuenn.

B. His outfield arm is among the greatest ever, and in 1965 he became the first outfielder ever to complete a season with no errors. He even pitched on two occasions.

C. He once hit four homers in a game at Baltimore's Memorial Stadium, a park which had never surrendered four home runs to any *team* in its existence up to that point.

59 A. In 1977 this slugger played for the Mets, Padres, Angels, and Yankees, to become the first man to play for and, in fact, homer for a team in each of big league baseball's then-existing four divisions in the same season.

B. In 1979 and 1982 he led the NL in homers, but he was notorious for his low batting average (.236 lifetime), substandard defense, and for striking out a bunch—11 times he finished in his league's top ten for whiffing, and he only played in more than 100 games in 12 seasons.

C. The 6-foot-6 outfielder/first baseman/third baseman/designated hitter *did* belt 442 home runs, but was frequently a baseball bad boy who once sent a dead rat to a writer.

60 A. From 1999 through 2013, this outfielder/first baseman carved out a name for himself, with 2006 being his best power year (45 HR, 136 RBIs, plus he hit .315). His highest batting average of .331 came in 2001.

B. In 2006 he joined Mickey Mantle as the only two switch-hitters to launch 40+ home runs in more than one season, and he was the 19th switch-hitter to jerk over 200 career homers.

C. Born in Waco, Texas, he's a product of Rice University who was drafted by the Houston Astros in the first round in 1997.

61 A. A first-round draft pick in 1994, this man played for the Padres, Marlins, Cubs, Braves, Orioles, and Pirates. He was involved in a trade for Kevin Brown and for Hee-Seop Choi.

B. He led the majors in hitting for the first half of 2005 at .376, and wound up leading the NL in batting at .335, hits, slugging, doubles with 50, total bases, and on-base plus slugging.

C. Ironically, his father was the major league scout said to have discovered Hee-Seop Choi. His uncle, Leron, also played big league ball.

62 A. This phenom broke onto the big league scene with a colossal splash, a veritable mania, in 1981 (after being up briefly in '80), racking up eight shutouts of his 13 victories in 25 starts.

B. He tied an All-Star record that had stood for 52 years when he fanned five straight AL hitters in 1986. Coincidentally, the two men who share this record both threw screwballs for their out pitch.

C. He won the Cy Young and the Rookie of the Year awards in 1981, a big league first.

63 A. When this player reported for the 1985 All-Star Game, he didn't have his Detroit uniform so he bought a souvenir replica jersey. Because that shirt didn't have a number on its back, he used a magic marker and inked his "1" onto the shirt.

B. The man who came to be known as "Sweet Lou" was the Rookie of the Year in 1978.

C. He and Alan Trammell formed a great double-play duo for an eon (1978–95), longer, in fact, than any other set of middle infielders.

64 A. This man set a record for pitching in the most games in a single season back in 1974 when he labored in 106 contests. No pitcher before or since has thrown in 100+ games, and no man has ever surpassed his 84 games finished (1979).

B. Additionally, in 1974, his Cy Young season, he established another mark by appearing in 13 straight games.

C. Due to his durability and, of course, his first name, it was inevitable for him to become known as "Iron Mike." Only he and the indefatigable Kent Tekulve appeared in 90+ games in three seasons.

65 A. A 300-game winner and Hall of Famer, this man shares the record for being in five World Series (pitching in all but one) without once winning a championship.

B. He only won 20 once, and was never impressive enough to win the Cy Young Award, but he did whiff 3,574 batters (number seven all time through 2019), aided, many say, by doctoring the baseball—thus, his nickname: "Black and Decker."

C. Most of his playing days were spent with the Dodgers, but he was in the 1982 World Series with the Brewers. While he never led his league in strikeouts, he was the first pitcher to whiff 100+ in 20 straight seasons.

66 A. In 2000 this controversial righty led the AL in ERA at 1.74, an incredible record 3.17 lower than the league average.

B. He began his career in Los Angeles, where his brother Ramon already had registered a 20-win season.

C. He's won three Cy Young Awards, two with the BoSox. He owns two 300+ K seasons, and his 2.81 lifetime ERA through 2006 made him the only then-active pitcher with an ERA below 3.00. His career ERA wound up at an impressive 2.93 and in 1999, when he won games at a .852 clip, he accomplished the pitchers' version of the Triple Crown.

67 A. This pitcher's nickname combined an adjective meaning "insane" and his nationality.

B. His trademark was his stomping around behind the mound and working himself into a frenzy prior to making a pitch.

C. The bulk of his career was spent with the Cardinals, where, in 1975, he led the NL in saves with a mere 22.

68 A. He is the only pitcher to throw a no-hitter which wrapped up a title, doing so in 1986, securing the NL West for his Astros.

B. That year he was on fire, winning the Cy Young Award while leading the league in strikeouts (306) and ERA (2.22).

C. Some attributed his success to his throwing scuffed baseballs; others sited his elusive, dipping splitter.

69 A. In the A's season finale of 1975, four pitchers combined for a no-hitter: Vida Blue, Glenn Abbott, Paul Lindblad, and Rollie Fingers. However, this pitcher is the only man to fire a perfect game in his team's final game of the season.

B. Most of his career was spent with the Angels, where he was an All-Star in 1986 and 1987.

C. The 6-foot-7 righty won a career high of 18 in 1986 when he came in third in the voting for the Cy Young Award.

70 A. In 1986 he set the record for dishing up the most homers, 50, in a season. Oddity: The homer he gave up to shoot by the old record came when he faced Jay Bell, one of three players this man had been traded for in 1985.

B. He possessed one of the greatest curves ever. Some say, with his 3,701 strikeouts and 287 wins, for a long time he was the best pitcher *not* in the Hall of Fame.

C. Born in Zeist, Holland, his full name is Rik Aalbert _____.

71 A. He was famous in college, at Michigan State University, where he was an All-American receiver (in fact, he was drafted by the NFL's St. Louis Cardinals), before gaining fame in the majors from 1979 to 1995.

B. Strangely, he won an MVP but never made an All-Star squad.

C. Finally, he hit one of the most famous and dramatic World Series home runs ever.

72 A. Speaking of college football, this man, an All-American running back, was the first player to appear in a Rose Bowl game (1949) and in a World Series (1950).

B. He retired at the age of 34, partly because of his aversion to air travel. Baseball had expanded to include teams on the

West Coast late in his career, and the long flights to and from Boston, where he played with the Red Sox, got to him.

C. He was the AL MVP in 1958.

73 A. Meanwhile, this man would leave baseball and go on to become a pro golfer. He is even credited by some sources as being the first man to wear a batting glove which was initially one of his golf gloves.

B. Later he became an announcer, mainly doing White Sox games. His nickname is the "Hawk."

C. He also had a stint as the White Sox general manager. In that capacity he fired field manager Tony La Russa.

74 A. In 2003, this man hit 42 of his 43 homers while working behind the plate, the most ever by a catcher in a season, eclipsing the mark held by Todd Hundley.

B. His best days were spent with the Braves, where he was an All-Star three times (even though he didn't usually catch when ace Greg Maddux was on the mound).

C. In 2004, he joined the Orioles and enjoyed another big year before fading; he was out of baseball by 2007. His sister Elaine was a professional volleyball player.

75 A. He is one of only six men to be on the winning side of a World Series as a manager (he did this in 1967), as a player (with the Cardinals and Braves), and as a coach (twice with St. Louis). On the debit side, in one capacity or another he was on the losing team three of the five times a club dropped the Series after holding down a three-games-to-one lead.

B. Until Ryne Sandberg outdid him, he held the highest fielding percentage in a season for a second baseman.

C. This Hall of Famer was the Cardinals' skipper from 1965 through 1976, the longest run in team history, until Tony La Russa came along.

○ ○ ○ **3** ○ ○ ○

ANSWERS

1 Bill Dickey

2 Carl "Yaz" Yastrzemski

3 Vernon Wells

4 Pepper Martin—and he was as "pungent" as pepper on the bases, driving opponents crazy with his base-path antics. When asked about his speed, he replied, "I grew up in Oklahoma, and once you start runnin' out there, there ain't nothin' to stop you." As a rookie, the colorful Martin reported late to spring training, explaining that he had been arrested for jumping a freight train. When his manager asked why he'd do such a thing when the club had given him railroad tickets, Martin replied, "What do you take me for, a dope? I cashed them in and rode for nothing."

5 Maury Wills

6 Steve Carlton. His 1972 ERA was a nearly invisible 1.97 over a now inconceivable 346 ⅓ innings of labor. Further, he fanned 310 men while walking only 87, and he even chipped in 30 complete games as he put together one of the most dominant pitching years ever. It was only natural that he won the Cy Young Award unanimously, making him the only pitcher from a last-place team to earn that trophy. That same year he also won more games in a row than any other pitcher on a last-place club—an amazing 15.

7 Bob Horner

8 Brian Roberts

9 Jose Vidro

10 Rick Monday, who had served six years in the Marine Reserves. The flag was later presented to him and proudly displayed in his home.

11 Andre Dawson. Later, Alex Rodriguez would join Dawson as the only men to win the MVP while playing for a last-place club.

12 Robert "Lefty" Grove. The $600 beyond the $100,000 figure that Dunn sold Grove to the Athletics for was tossed in by design to make this sale the largest, going beyond the often-stated $100,000 price tag for Ruth when he was sold from the Red Sox to the Yankees.

13 J. T. Snow

14 Billy Ripken. He, along with his brother, Cal Jr., make up one of only four brother "acts" to man the shortstop and second-base positions on the same team in the big leagues. The others were twin brothers Eddie and Johnny O'Brien for the Pirates, Garvin and Granny Hamner of the Phillies, and Frank Bolling and his brother Milt with the Tigers.

15 Walter Young. Although such records aren't exactly official, Young is said to be the first 300-pounder to reach the majors. Previously the man believed to be the heaviest was Jumbo Brown, listed at 295 pounds and labeled "the man who swallowed a taxicab."

16 Gene Garber

17 Dale Murphy

18 Steve Sax

19 Billy Wagner

20 Aaron Harang

21 Ellis Burks

22 Davey Johnson

23 Jeff Kent

24 Matty Alou. His brothers were, of course, Felipe and Jesus.

25 Jeff Bagwell. Oddity: In 1994 he was the NL MVP while Frank Thomas won that honor in the AL—the two men were both first basemen and had been born on the same day, May 27, 1968, just nine and a half hours apart. No two teammates clubbed more combined doubles than "Bags" and Craig Biggio (1,110).

26 Albert Belle

27 Fred McGriff

28 Jon Matlack

29 Larry Walker. He was the first Canadian to win the MVP, and he owns more homers than any other Canadian in the majors.

30 Bobby Bonds

31 Mike Hargrove

32 Joe Medwick. He was the first man to homer in the All-Star Game and the World Series in the same season, 1934.

33 Mookie Wilson. It was, of course, his ground ball, a mere dribbler, that went through the legs of Boston's first baseman Bill Buckner in Game 6 of the '86 Series that won it all for the Mets.

34 David Ortiz

35 Tommy John. His surgery, performed by the renowned Dr. Frank Jobe, replaced the ulnar collateral ligament in his throwing arm with a tendon from his right forearm.

36 Ken Griffey Sr. Not only did he and "Junior" become teammates in Seattle, but they also set other father-son "firsts" when they both collected a hit in the same game and when they both homered in the same contest.

37 Dave Concepcion

38 Grady Sizemore

39 Jim Thome

40 Darin Erstad

41 Rennie Stennett. The record for the most hits in a big league game regardless of innings played is nine by Cleveland's Johnny

Burnett, who pounded out those record hits over an 18-inning contest back in 1932.

42 Jack Clark

43 Bill Mazeroski

44 Nate Colbert

45 Ron Darling. He was well known for his intelligence. His mother was part Chinese and his father was part French; Ron spoke both those languages fluently.

46 Torii Hunter

47 Rob Deer

48 Terry Francona

49 Richie Ashburn

50 Mark Whiten

51 Richie "Dick" Allen. He is the first AL MVP to wear glasses.

52 Rick Sutcliffe. "The Red Baron" had also won the Rookie of the Year Award when he broke in with the Dodgers.

53 Bartolo Colon

54 Nomar Garciaparra. In 1997, his 30 homers set a record for the most home runs by a rookie shortstop, and his 98 RBIs were the most ever by a leadoff hitter.

55 Norm Cash

56 Matt Williams

57 Hoyt Wilhelm

58 Rocky Colavito

59 Dave Kingman

60 Lance Berkman

61 Derrek Lee

62 Fernando Valenzuela

63 Lou Whitaker

64 Mike Marshall

65 Don Sutton

66 Pedro Martinez

67 Al Hrabosky, "The Mad Hungarian"

68 Mike Scott

69 Mike Witt

70 Bert Blyleven

71 Kirk Gibson

72 Jackie Jensen. His wife, by the way, was Zoe Ann Olsen, who won a silver medal in diving during the 1948 Summer Olympics.

73 Ken Harrelson

74 Javy Lopez

75 Red Schoendienst

○ ○ ○ **4** ○ ○ ○

THE STRETCH INNINGS

1 A. This man's career was fleeting; he won the American League Rookie of the Year Award in 1980, and just 70 games later, played over a two-year span, he was through.

   B. He was widely known for his many wild antics, such as opening beer bottles with his eye sockets.

   C. He was a Cleveland outfielder and his initials are "J.C."

2 A. This man was a big league manager, left to join the ranks of college coaches at the University of South Alabama, and later accepted the job of running the Texas Rangers in 1977, only to quit that position after just one day on the job; he cited homesickness as the reason for handing in his resignation.

   B. As a player—he was an infielder, mainly a second baseman—he was far from being a quitter; he was a scrappy, feisty ballplayer. In fact, Leo Durocher once said of this man, "He can't hit, he can't run, he can't throw—all he can do is beat you."

   C. He was dubbed "The Brat" partly due to his pesky ways; he drew a ton of walks and hit a modest .268 over 11 years, but with a fine on-base percentage of .410.

3 A. This man, a sparkplug of a player, was a member of the world champion 1986 Mets (in fact, he broke in with the Mets in 1980 and stayed there through 1988). Bobby Bonilla, a teammate of this man later in Pittsburgh, spoke of how valuable this player was, saying all winning teams need "a guy who, when the phone rings in the middle of the night, you say, 'Oh, no, I hope he's not in trouble.'" Such players, he felt, stir things up, keep a team loose, and contribute highly to successful teams.

B. Like the man discussed in the previous question, this man also had a very short tenure as a big league manager. As a matter of fact, he was hired on November 1, 2004, to lead the Arizona Diamondbacks, only to be fired four days later, before he had even had the opportunity to meet with his players. The team had failed to run a background check on him, but when press reports exposed run-ins with the law—a DWI charge in 2000, and allegations of domestic violence—the D-backs quickly axed him.

C. A .275 lifetime hitter, he was primarily a second baseman, but played over 100 games at third base, too.

4 A. Barry Zito's lucrative contract was discussed in Chapter 1 of this book, but what player had held the record for the largest contract for a pitcher prior to Zito? Clues: He was coming off a couple of fine seasons in 1999 (with a stellar 22–4 record for the Houston Astros) and 2000 (15–10 as a member of the New York Mets), then signed with the Colorado Rockies where he fizzled, going 21–28 over the subsequent two seasons.

B. In 2003 and 2004, this lefty rebounded a bit, going 27–17 for Atlanta under manager Bobby Cox and his wizard of a pitching coach, Leo Mazzone. However, he did not pitch in 2006 and 2007, and went 10–14 over his final three seasons.

C. A fine hitter and fielder, he won five Silver Slugger Awards and one Gold Glove; former teammate Jeff Bagwell called him, along with Greg Maddux, the best fielding pitchers he had ever seen.

5 A. This left-handed pitcher, who lasted from 1984 through 1996, shares an unusual first name with that of a popular writer of tales of the Old West.

B. He won 100 games while toiling for the Braves, Expos, Pirates, and, briefly, the Red Sox with his personal zenith of 16 wins coming in 1991.

C. This man's surname is the most common last name in the United States.

6 A. Good hitters often say that when they're in the groove, the ball appears to be as large as a grapefruit to them. Well, this man's blazing fastball came in looking as tiny as a cherry tomato. Once, when the legendary Walter Johnson, also known as "The Big Train" (a precursor to the equally fitting moniker for Nolan Ryan, The Ryan Express), was asked to compare his fastball to that of the man in question, stated, "Listen, mister, no man alive can throw any harder than _____."

B. He pitched for the Red Sox from 1908 through 1915 before an injury cost him the 1916 season. He notched 34 wins in 1912 and went 3–1 in that year's World Series, but managed only 117 career wins, good for a lustrous .672 won-loss percentage.

C. In 1918, he converted to the outfield and finished in the top ten for batting average, doubles, homers, runs driven in, and extra base hits. He would go on to coach at Yale.

7 A. According to UPI sports writer Milton Richman, this pitcher (whose real first name was Jim) took a stand during spring training of 1967, trying to "become the first modern major leaguer to wear a beard while playing ball during the regular season."

B. While pitching for the Twins in the 1965 World Series versus the Dodgers, he became the first American League African American to chisel out a win in Series play. That same season The Sporting News selected him as their AL Pitcher of the Year.

C. His nickname comes from a fish and is also the nickname of a minor league baseball team located near Raleigh, North Carolina.

8 A. After leaving the playing fields, this popular man became an announcer for the Angels. Over his career which ran from

1984 to 1998, he played every position on the diamond except pitching and catching.
B. His first name is the Latin word for "king." For that matter, it's also the first name of one of the starting quarterbacks in the Super Bowl of February 4, 2007, and can also be found in the second part of the name of the "king" of the dinosaurs.
C. His nickname was "Wonder Dog."

9 A. This man shares his last name with that of a famous British director who was so skilled and popular, he was knighted.
B. The former pitcher's first name could be an adjective describing a type of silver or something that conforms to the highest standard.
C. He broke in with the Yankees in 1992 and lasted through 2004, also spending time with the Mariners, where he won a career-high 13 games in 1996; the Padres, where he got his first taste of World Series play; and, briefly, with the Cardinals.

10 A. The winner of the 1950 AL Rookie of the Year Award, this 6-foot-5 slugger, who broke in as a member of the Boston Red Sox, made the All-Star team his first season, but never again over his 13 big league seasons.
B. Sixty-three of his 152 career homers came in his first two seasons in which he chalked up 500 or more at bats, 1950 and 1952. After '52 he would never again hit more than 19 homers, and would only reach double digits in home runs three more times.
C. His greatest glory may well be a record streak he amassed when he once banged out 12 straight hits over two days.

11 A. This player is part of a three-generation baseball family, and, as a play on words tying in with his last name, his nickname was "Ding Dong."
B. His career spanned 15 seasons (1950–64), mainly with the Reds. He hit a solid .281 with some punch and made four All-Star squads.

C. His grandsons, David and Mike, debuted in the majors in 1995 and 2000 respectively. Mike lasted 19 games while David was still active until 2006.

12 A. This man is also a member of a three-generation baseball family and played from 1972 through 1990.

B. He played primarily for the Phillies, and then the Angels, and was a four-time All-Star. When he played in his final season he was 42 years old, making him the second-oldest player in the majors at the time and one of the oldest catchers ever.

C. Among catchers only Ivan Rodriguez with 13, Johnny Bench, who had 10, and Yadier Molina with 9, own more Gold Glove Awards than this man's seven.

13 A. In college, this player gained a great deal of renown on the gridiron as a receiver for a major football "factory," playing his final game during the 2006 season (bowing out with a loss to LSU in the Sugar Bowl, where he hauled in a touchdown pass). He was, according to an Associated Press report, projected as a first-round [NFL] pick.

B. Instead of football, this right-handed pitcher signed a five-year deal with the Cubs worth $10 million in January of 2007. He had been the Cubs' fifth-round pick in the 2006 amateur draft, and started seven games for two Cubs minor league teams, posting a 2.70 ERA.

C. Up from the farm system in 2008, he registered an ERA of 2.28, bolstering the Cubs bullpen. By 2019, he was with the Giants, but by season's end his record, mainly as a starter, was a less than commendable 80–104.

14 A. After spending time with the Padres, Phillies, Orioles, and Mets, in 2008 this journeyman signed his final big league contract with the Astros. Primarily an outfielder, he was versatile enough to play every position on the diamond besides pitcher, catcher, and shortstop during his eight-year stint in the majors.

B. At first many felt he was, at 5-foot-10 and 180 pounds, too small to play big league ball, and he did languish in the minors for years.

C. His father, whose first name is Ross, is a baseball writer for the *Los Angeles Times* and is honored at Cooperstown in the Hall of Fame.

15 A. The words that best describe this pitcher, who spent 1997 through 2005 with the Cardinals before signing with the Giants as a free agent, are *dependable, control artist, workhorse*, and *underrated*. He worked the last month of the 2006 season, his first of just two seasons with a sub-.500 record, with broken ribs. He spent his final season, 2008, with the Pirates.

B. A first-round pick in the 1995 draft, he won in double digits in eight of his first 10 seasons, he wound up with 121 career wins, and posted a .568 won-loss percentage.

C. His most impressive season had to be 2001 when he went 22–8—his win total led the league—with a glistening ERA of 3.16.

16 A. In 1988 this right-handed pitcher was sizzling hot. He capped his sensational 23–8 season (with a 2.26 ERA) by being named the MVP of the World Series, making him the first man ever to win the Cy Young Award (doing so unanimously) and the MVP of both the Fall Classic *and* his league's Championship Series in the same season.

B. That year he also put together a marvelous, record-setting streak by firing 59 consecutive shutout innings (to break the mark set by Don Drysdale). In September of 1988 alone he registered five shutouts, but his whitewash skein ended after just ⅓ of an inning at the start of the next season.

C. His manager, Tommy Lasorda, gave him the nickname "Bulldog" because he felt his star pitcher was so tenacious.

17 A. At one time in the 1960s (*circa* 1967), the Philadelphia Phillies had a lineup which included three men at the bottom third of the order with these surnames: White, Wine, and Boozer. The first baseman was Bill White, who later went on to become the NL president; and John Boozer was a pitcher—who according to one report, once was tossed from a game *before* it began, caught throwing spitballs during his warm-up by the umpire. Can you supply the first name of the player named Wine?

B. His career began in 1960 with Philadelphia, and he endured through the 1972 season. He went from the Phils to the Expos in the expansion draft of 1969.

C. Normally a slick shortstop who owned one Gold Glove, he committed a career high of 31 errors in the Expos' inaugural season.

18 A. He was the type of defensive outfielder that made fans react as if they were watching fireworks go off, muttering repeatedly, "Oooh. Ahh." An eight-time Gold Glove winner, his nickname was "The Secretary of Defense," and an announcer once said of his range, "Two-thirds of the earth is covered by water; the other one-third is covered by _____."

B. He began with the Giants in 1972, and was traded to Philadelphia where he stayed (and gained most of his ink) for the rest of his 15-year career.

C. In America's bicentennial year, he finished fifth in the voting for the MVP trophy when he hit a career high .330.

19 A. Until Tim Raines was admitted into the Hall of Fame in 2017, the next man in question was the only member of the Hall whose first name was Tim, gaining Fame status in 1964 when the Veterans Committee voted him in.

B. He is an obscure name because he labored in the early, dark days of the game—he was a submarine pitcher whose career ran from 1880 through 1893. However, he did win 341 contests over those 14 seasons, twice won 40 or more games, and was victorious a record 19 straight times in 1888.

C. Remarkably, on the Fourth of July back in 1883, he worked both ends of a doubleheader, winning and going the distance in both affairs, and surrendering just three hits all day.

20 A. A genius with the leather and with unlimited range, when this infielder got his glove on the ball, it was secured, snatched with the authority of a gator's chomp. In fact, other than Brooks Robinson and two pitchers, no man has ever won more Gold Glove Awards than this man.

B. He broke in with a West Coast club in 1978, but his greatest years came with a club in the Midwest.

C. Early on this switch-hitter's bat was lackluster—at times he even hovered in the vicinity of the Mendoza Line—but he turned himself into a solid stick and even won one Silver Slugger Award (1987). He also swatted a memorable home run off Tom Niedenfuer in the 1985 NLCS, his first home run as a lefty.

21 A. A great fielding pitcher, this southpaw won more Gold Glove Awards than any man ever until 2007, when Greg Maddux won his 17th trophy for fielding excellence.

B. Despite winning nearly 300 games (283 over 25 seasons), Hall of Fame voters have shunned him.

C. The 1966 Pitcher of the Year, as selected by *The Sporting News*, this man found ways of enduring in the bigs. For example, late in his career he became a quick pitch artist to keep much younger batters off stride. He lasted until he was 44, and, from 1976 (when he was 37 years old) through 1983, he was among the five oldest players in the majors.

22 A. This man, primarily a fine third baseman (although he began his major league career at shortstop) with a strong and sure arm, was born on America's Independence Day, but in Oaxaca, Mexico.

B. He began his big league days with Atlanta, and returned there late in his career, but he put up his biggest numbers—including consecutive seasons of 40, 40, and a personal high of 46 homers—in Colorado. He officially announced his retirement early in 2007.

C. He owns 320 lifetime homers, and his home-run total, as well as his career hits, runs, and doubles totals, ranked first among Mexican-born ballplayers.

23 A. This pitcher of the 1950s and 1960s passed away in early 2007. He belongs to an elite group of men that won three games in a World Series. He also went the distance against Harvey Haddix the night Haddix threw 12 innings of perfect baseball.

B. The Yankees, who originally signed him and worked him in only two big league contests, must have regretted trading him to the Braves when the righty went 3–0 with two shutouts and an invisible ERA of 0.67 against them in the 1957 Fall Classic. His final 24 innings against the Yankees were all scoreless.

C. He was known as "Nitro," but not for, say, possessing an explosive fastball, but because he hailed from the town of Nitro, West Virginia.

24 A. This man also nailed down three wins in a World Series even though another pitcher on the staff was considered to be the team's ace—deservedly so, because the number-one man remains the last pitcher to win 30 games in a season.

B. The pitcher in question was with the Tigers from 1963 through 1975, and rang up 217 wins.

C. He had a cousin, Ron, who also played in the majors.

25 A. This former Pittsburgh Pirates and St. Louis Cardinals standout was a two-time All-American college basketball player.

B. He won the 1960 batting crown and the NL MVP, hitting .325 while leading the Pirates to the world championship.

C. His college hoop fame came at Duke; in 1952, his jersey was the first to be retired at that university, and they would not honor another player thusly until 1980. He also spent one season with the Fort Wayne Pistons in the NBA.

26 A. This player, who played in his 19th season in 2019, has put up simply fantastic numbers. His *average* season (when based on his playing a full 162-game season) produces 184 hits, 38

doubles, 38 homers, 119 runs driven in, 105 runs, and a .300 batting average.

B. In February of 2007, he made headlines when he scored a perfect 100 on his United States citizenship test. He continues to make news and milestones—he now has 3,202 hits and 656 HR. If he finishes his career with a .300+ batting average, only he, Willie Mays, and Hank Aaron would be lifetime .300 hitters who are also in the 3,000 hit/600 HR club.

C. In 2006, he became the first player to boast of 30 or more homers and 100+ RBI in each of his first six seasons while also becoming the youngest big leaguer to reach the 250 home run mark. He kept his 30+ HR with 100+ RBI streak alive all the way until 2011, when he fell just one RBI shy of reaching the 20/100 levels for the 11th straight year.

27 A. This powerful first baseman of the 1950s and 1960s was, in 1953, the first of three men (Hank Aaron and Lou Brock would follow nine years later—with their long balls coming *on consecutive days*) to power a ball into the center-field bleachers at the old Polo Grounds.

B. Along with Aaron, Eddie Mathews, and Frank Thomas, he formed a quartet of Braves who became the first players ever to connect on back-to-back-to-back-to-*back* home runs on June 8, 1961.

C. For almost half a century he held the record for the most total bases in a single game when he lashed out four homers and a double against the Dodgers on July 31, 1954, good for a staggering 18 total bases. When Harvey Haddix fired his perfect game in 1959, this man was the first to get a hit off him—in the 13th inning (the "perfect" status was later removed from Haddix's game in the official record books).

28 A. This outfielder broke the single-game record for total bases with 19 when, on May 24, 2002, he belted out four homers and threw in a double and a single for good measure, going 6-for-6 versus the Milwaukee Brewers.

B. His big day came in the Dodgers uniform, but he broke in with the Blue Jays in 1993, and has also spent time with the Diamondbacks and the Mets.

C. He reached 40 or more home runs on three occasions (two times with the Dodgers), and twice he was an All-Star.

29 A. This big leaguer played at Westminster Christian School along with Alex Rodriguez.

B. His career spanned 1998 to 2009 with seven clubs, but his finest years were spent in the uniform of the Minnesota Twins, where he won a Gold Glove in 2001 for his nifty work at first base.

C. His last name is so long and difficult to spell, he was given the nickname "Eye Chart."

30 A. A hard-throwing reliever, this Caracas, Venezuela, native experienced his best period of success from 1997 through 1999, when he piled up 102 saves. In 1998, he recorded a microscopic 1.30 ERA for the Expos.

B. His first and last name both start with the same vowel.

C. He was arrested in his home country on November 7, 2005, on a charge of attempted murder. Earlier, when he was with the Tigers, he had to leave the team to go to Venezuela when his mother was kidnapped and a $6 million ransom was demanded.

31 A. For years he held the record for the most times being plunked by a pitch for a career (243). In 1971, his first year with the Expos, he was hit 50 times, a modern-day record that still stands. The player who came in second for the most times hit by a pitch (HBP) that year was his teammate, Rusty Staub, who was drilled only nine times. This man may have only hit .279 that season, but his on-base percentage was, at .402, among the league leaders.

B. He would intentionally wear his uniform shirt baggy, hoping that a pitch might nick his jersey and earn him yet another free ride to first base.

C. A second baseman by trade, he made two All-Star teams, both times as a member of the Mets.

32 A. This is a very difficult one: In 1969, this third baseman was a rookie for the expansion Montreal Expos, a team that mainly fielded castoffs and marginal players such as John Boccabella, but with a few future stars such as Staub tossed in.

B. The player in question bolted out of the starting gate, was hitting a lusty .377 by the end of April, and had prompted some serious hype—an All-Star berth seemed feasible for this no-name youngster. He did, in fact, wind up second in the balloting for the Rookie of the Year Award (.258 with 83 RBIs), but quickly tapered off after his torrid start, hitting a miserable .173 in May and .173 from September 1 through the end of the season.

C. Just three years later, he played in only 28 games, then 22, then oblivion. Perhaps what most fans recall about him was his unusual first name, the same one as an outfielder who enjoyed two fine seasons in 2004 and 2005 with the Indians before moving on to the Red Sox to replace Johnny Damon the following year.

33 A. Another tough one from the past. Like the Indians/Red Sox player mentioned above, this man's nickname is also food-related, having a connection with a breakfast cereal; his nickname was "Sugar Bear."

B. Playing from 1972 through 1980, mainly with Atlanta and Cleveland, he was pretty much a marginal player who hit .252 lifetime.

C. A cynic might say his last name is what he was "shooting," as, again, he wasn't much of a hitter, good only for about five homers and 44 RBIs per 162 games played.

34 A. This pitcher's biggest claim to fame (or infamy) stems from his being rushed to the big leagues, at the age of 18, directly out of high school. Despite his highly touted potential, his career never panned out. As a matter of fact, he flopped, going 18–33 lifetime over five seasons.

B. Like other hurlers who gained much early hype, such as Mark Fidrych, Vida Blue, and Fernando Valenzuela, this man—the first person selected in the 1973 draft—drew huge crowds—in his case to Texas Rangers contests. In fact, he won his first start in front of a sellout crowd. Unfortunately, because he was unfairly thrust too quickly into the majors, the crowds and his career soon faded.

C. In fact, this southpaw's days were done, due to injuries, by the time he had turned 26.

35 A. This man was to Brooks Robinson what Babe Dahlgren was to Lou Gehrig in that when Robinson faded, he was replaced at third base by this player.

B. Ironically, he was later traded by the O's to the Angels in order to make room for a promising youngster by the name of Cal Ripken Jr., who played both third and short. Ripken manned third base 77 times early on in his career and returned there late in his playing days.

C. This one-time All-Star enjoyed his finest year with the Angels in 1982 when he established career highs of .301, 30 HR, and 97 RBIs while finishing third in the MVP balloting.

36 A. When it was Ripken's turn to hang up his spikes, Tony Batista replaced him at third base. However, a few years earlier in 1997, when the time had come for Ripken to give up his starting shortstop slot, he did so to this smooth fielder.

B. This man's career spanned from 1990 through 2003, with one of his biggest highlights being his record streak of 110 games and 543 consecutive errorless chances in 2002.

C. He was an All-Star in 2000, but because he played in the same league with shortstops such as Omar Vizquel, he was denied a Gold Glove despite his steady, but not especially flashy, glove.

37 A. He was the first player ever to connect for home runs on his first two at-bats in World Series play, doing so in 1972 when half

of his eight hits (.348) went for homers which, along with his nine runs driven in, helped him earn the MVP trophy of that Series.

B. He was a catcher/first baseman and was an integral part of the Oakland A's dynasty that secured three consecutive World Series titles from 1972 to 1974.

C. His real first name is Fury, and his last name is pronounced the same way as a sport which, like baseball, requires its players to strike a ball with a piece of equipment.

38 A. In 2006, this AL Central slugger, despite playing in only 129 games, crushed 42 homers, including six grand slams, which tied the single-season record set by Don Mattingly in 1987.

B. He has a most unusual nickname: "Pronk," a combination of the words "project" and "donkey."

C. Although he became the first player ever to swat five grand slams by the All-Star break, he was not named to the All-Star squad that year, 2006.

39 A. This player won both a Gold Glove and a Silver Slugger Award in 2005 for an AL Western Division club, and took home another Gold Glove trophy in 2006.

B. Through his first six seasons (2003–08), he averaged nearly 35 homers per season, and he went berserk with the bat in 2005 with 144 RBIs, a single-season record by a switch-hitter. That same season he joined Eddie Murray and Chipper Jones as the only switch-hitters to hit 20 or more homers in each of their first three years in the majors. In fact, aside from his 26-homer and 84-RBI season as a rookie, he hit 30+ HR and drove home 100+ every season until 2012.

C. Further, at one point it was reported that only he and four other men—all luminaries: Joe DiMaggio, Ralph Kiner, Eddie Mathews, and Albert Pujols—had ever teed off for 100+ home runs during their first three big-league seasons..

40 A. This man had a strong Ohio connection all of his life. He was born in 1947 in Canton, attended Kent State University,

and died at the age of just 32 in Canton, where he had grown up.

B. His jersey number (15) was retired by the Yankees in 1979 shortly after his death. He remains the only Yankee to win both the Rookie of the Year Award and an MVP (1976).

C. In the '76 World Series, he hit a blistering .529, spanking out a record-tying six straight hits at one point, albeit in a losing cause versus the Reds.

41 A. The winner of the 1960 Cy Young Award, this righty was an All-Star only once, in '60, when his team won the World Series.

B. Due to his religious ways—he was a devout Mormon—he earned the nickname "Deacon."

C. His son, Vance, also made it to the big leagues, mainly playing third base.

42 A. Drawing an intentional walk with the bases loaded is very rare, but this Hall of Famer (Class of '37) once was given such respect. He played more than 2,000 games at second base from 1896 through 1916.

B. At one time the Cleveland franchise took its nickname from this man's first name, a huge tribute to his ability and popularity.

C. He won five batting titles, hitting his high-water mark of .426 in 1901, when he won a Triple Crown, albeit with only 14 home runs. He won the crown by a record 149 points over his league's average, and outhit his nearest rival by a record 86 points.

43 A. This infielder, who played from 1996 to 2007, attended Louisiana State University, where he shattered that school's record for RBI, which had been held by Albert Belle.

B. His most prolific season was probably 2003, when he was the starting second baseman for the Red Sox (92 runs, 85 RBIs), his only year with that club.

C. That year his productivity carried over into the postseason as he hit .312 against Oakland in the ALDS, then an even more potent .370 versus the Yankees in the next round.

44 A. On May 2, 1917, the Cubs and Reds squared off in what became a classic confrontation. When the ninth inning ended, both Cincinnati's Fred Toney and Hippo Vaughn of the Cubs had no-hitters going. The affair ended in 10 innings when this man's infield hit (after a one-out single had, moments earlier, broken up Vaughn's half of the "double no-hitter") ultimately sent the Reds home with a win, and with Toney able to cling to his "no-no."

B. The man in question, of Native American heritage, is actually better known for his football and Olympic accomplishments. During the closing ceremonies of the 1912 Olympic Games, King Gustav V of Sweden called this star, who had copped gold medals in both the pentathlon and the decathlon, "the greatest athlete in the world." He is, in fact, one of seven men enshrined in the Pro Football Hall of Fame who also played big league baseball.

C. Because it came to light in 1913 that he had spent some time (and made a few dollars) playing pro baseball in 1909 and 1910, he was officially declared to be a professional athlete and was therefore stripped of his Olympic medals. He then went on to spend six years, but only 698 at-bats, in the majors, where he hit a lackluster .252, supporting the contention that hitting a baseball is the single most difficult skill in all of sports.

45 A. When he was 50 days shy of his 16th birthday, this popular Cincinnati figure became the youngest player ever to appear on a big league diamond. During 1944, a World War II season in which a great deal of major league talent had been siphoned away from the ball fields, sent to serve their country on distant fields, this pitcher made his big league debut.

B. A good ol' Joe, he was a two-time All-Star (1955 and 1956), but never won more than 17 games in a given season.

C. After his playing days were over, he became an announcer for the Reds, closing his day's broadcasting duties with his trademark farewell: "This is the old left-hander rounding third and heading for home."

46 A. This slugger is most famous for his tenure with the New York Yankees. He broke in with them in 1954 and stayed there through 1962 as their first sacker.

B. Over that span he was part of a pennant-winning team seven times, and, when he was traded to the Dodgers for the 1963 season, he again went to the World Series, sweeping the Yankees while hitting a lofty .385.

C. His real first name is Bill, but he went by a nickname—the name of a large and powerful animal.

47 A. In the 1972 NLCS, this pitcher couldn't get out of the first inning of Game 2. In fact, he didn't even record a single out, surrendering four runs to the Reds. In the ninth inning of the finale, he gave the Reds the pennant when his wild pitch brought home the game-winning run.

B. His last name is the same as the nickname of the man from the previous question.

C. The finest year of his 10-year career was 1969, when he went 14–3 with a no-hitter and an ERA of 2.91 as a 21-year-old with the Pirates.

48 A. He is a Texas native, growing up there just like two of his role models, both big strikeout artists.

B. He was the fourth player selected in the 1995 amateur draft. By 2003, he led the NL in strikeouts. In 1998, he led the list for the best ratio of strikeouts per nine innings with a scorching 12.58 mark. It was little wonder he won the Rookie of the Year Award back then.

C. Without being specific enough to give this one away, this man's greatest single outing produced a slew of strikeouts—in just his fifth career start—frustrating many an Astros batter in a fabulous one-hitter. In 2007, he was converted into a reliever and he never again started a game.

49 A. During the 1985 NLCS, this man made headlines when he was trapped under a motorized, automatic tarp in St. Louis while he was doing his pregame stretching. The injury he sustained to his leg kept him out of the rest of the series.

B. Over his career he swiped 752 bases, led the NL in steals each year over his first six seasons, and set a personal high with a magnificent total, 110, as a rookie. Needless to say, he breezed to the Rookie of the Year Award as a unanimous selection.

C. His cousin Greg Coleman was the first African-American punter in the NFL.

50 A. A former player for, most notably, the Phillies and Cardinals, this man went on to become the president of the National League.

B. In 1964, when the Cards won the World Series over the Yankees, this man finished third in the voting for the NL MVP.

C. His last name is the same as a color.

51 A. An outfielder with a reputation for being surly to the media and hard to manage, this man won the AL batting title in 1970 when he hit .329, his lifetime best.

B. His brother Ron was a football standout. He received the sixth-highest vote total for the 1968 Heisman Trophy and went on to star in the NFL for the Cleveland Browns and the New York Giants.

C. This player's last name is the same as that of an American president who went by "LBJ."

52 A. This man, despite once hitting over 60 home runs in the minors (66 HR in Class "A" back in 1956), was perhaps best known for his porous glove; he was given the nickname "Dr. Strangeglove."

B. "Errors are a part of my image," he once stated. "One night in Pittsburgh, 30,000 fans gave me a standing ovation when I caught a hot-dog wrapper on the fly."

C. Five times he finished in the top ten in his league for home runs (1958–69).

53 A. This outfielder got married in 1999, just three days before he was selected as the AL Rookie of the Year. Back then, he wore the Royals uniform.

B. When he became a free agent after a scintillating 2004 season—he hit .455 and .417 respectively in the NLDS (in which he added four homers and nine RBIs versus Atlanta) and the NLCS (he blasted four more home runs)—he was coveted by the Mets. He didn't click at first, but in 2006 he set personal bests for walks, homers, runs, and ribbies.

C. In 2006, he even took home his first of three Gold Gloves, patrolling center field almost flawlessly (only two errors) while racking up 13 assists. In 2019, he was named manager for the following season for a team he once played for.

54 A. He has done it all: He played in the majors for nine seasons, mainly with Texas; he was the Rangers' general manager; and he spent 2019 in the Rangers broadcast booth—his 25th season providing color commentary.

B. His son Ben went from being a Texas batboy to becoming the 1998 AL Rookie of the Year when he also made the All-Star squad representing the Oakland A's.

C. Most of his playing days were spent in the outfield. When he was the Rangers GM, he made some fine moves, like acquiring Rafael Palmeiro and Jamie Moyer, but he also engineered the trade that sent Sammy Sosa to the Cubs.

55 A. This former star pitcher (1968–79), who experienced his best years primarily with the Angels and Dodgers, followed the path paved by Curt Flood and was instrumental in baseball's loss of the reserve clause when arbitrator Peter Seitz made a 1975 ruling in favor of the pitcher. Long story short, due to the pitcher's case (actually *pitchers'* case—his co-complainant was Dave McNally), the age of free agency swooped onto the baseball scene.

B. He was a 20-game winner twice and led his league in shutouts, made four All-Star teams, and won two Gold Glove Awards.

C. When he went to Atlanta in 1976, team owner Ted Turner slapped the unlikely nickname of "Channel" on him and had him wear that name on jersey #17 (until NL president Chub Feeney disallowed this gimmick). Turner's purpose was to advertise his station which carried Braves games. Every time this pitcher would appear, he'd be a walking billboard for Channel 17, Turner's WTBS SuperStation number.

56 A. Tough one: This man was the last pitcher to throw a *legal* spitball, doing so in 1934, ten years after the unsanitary pitch had been outlawed.

B. This 270-game winner's nickname reflected his appearance, as he loved to sport intimidating facial hair when he took to the mound. His nickname? "Ol' Stubblebeard."

C. He was intimidating in more ways than one, and reportedly threw at a hitter—while he was still in the on-deck circle. He was inducted into the Hall of Fame in 1964. His initials are "B.G."

57 A. This knuckleball pitcher spent 1961 to 1978 in the majors and is the last man to start both ends of a doubleheader, achieving that rare feat on July 20, 1973, with the White Sox.

B. Throwing effortlessly, he pushed at the 400-innings-pitched envelope in 1972. That year, *The Sporting News* named him their Pitcher of the Year based largely on his 24–17 record. The year before he logged his best ERA ever as a starter, 1.91.

C. The initials of his first and last names are the same letter.

58 A. After the 2006 season, this popular outfielder left the team he had spent the last eight seasons with to play for the Dodgers, before moving on to the Marlins in 2008 to conclude his 19 years in the majors. He may have been pushing 40, but in 2006 he put up a career-high 52 doubles, becoming the oldest player with 50+ doubles in a season.

B. The father of triplets, this Tampa native was drafted by Houston and debuted in 1990. When he drastically changed his batting stance, good things began to happen. In 2001, he peppered 57 homers—his previous personal high had been 31.

C. He won the 2001 Home Run Derby held prior to the All-Star Game and, much more importantly, capped off a great season by unknotting a 2–2 tie in Game 7 of the World Series. His bases-loaded blooper off Yankees star Mariano Rivera secured the Series for Arizona.

59 A. Virtually unknown prior to 2006, he became a nova at the start of 2006, smoking nine homers over his first 13 contests, making him the fastest player in AL history to hit that many homers that quickly.

B. However, he inevitably slowed down, and his team sent him to Toledo to make room for the newly acquired Sean Casey.

C. He did reemerge briefly with Texas in 2008 before ending his days with Seattle in 2009. After his initial power outburst, he wound up with just 28 more homers, giving him 37 lifetime homers.

60 A. This reliever won 22 games in a row from 1958 to 1959 for the Pittsburgh Pirates.

B. Relying on his fine forkball, he went 17–0 to start the 1959 season before he finally dropped a decision. He finished the year at 18–1, giving him a .947 won-loss percentage, the best ever among pitchers with 15+ decisions. His 18 relief wins is still a record.

C. In the 1960 World Series he became the first pitcher to chalk up three saves.

61 A. While he was a very solid pitcher for 18 seasons, he was no match for Steve Carlton, yet the two men were traded for one another in 1972.

B. When he authored his 1971 no-hitter for the Phillies, he supplied most of the firepower in his own support, hitting a two-run homer and a solo shot in a 4–0 win. No other pitcher has ever accomplished that.

C. He made his big league debut as an 18-year-old in 1964. He once won 19 and enjoyed a season in which he posted an ERA of 2.88.

62 A. He was the only man ever to win a Triple Crown and then get traded the following season. In 1933, as a Phillies outfielder, he put up phenomenal numbers (.368, 28 HR, 120 RBIs) but was sent packing to the Cubs in the off-season.

B. He won the 1932 NL MVP, led his league in homers and total bases four times, and three times in slugging percentage.

C. His 44 assists in his second full season, 1930, remains the most ever by a modern-day outfielder. Somehow it took until 1980, 36 years after he had played his last game, for the .320 lifetime hitter to become a Hall of Famer.

63 A. His given name at birth was Aloysius Szymanski. A Hall of Fame outfielder, he swatted 307 HR, and is best remembered for his days with the Philadelphia A's.

B. He hit .334 lifetime, going beyond .380 four times. In his second season, 1925, he hit .387; two years later he soared to .392. Later he would finally win batting crowns with .381 and .390 averages.

C. Because of his unique batting style, he was known as "Bucketfoot Al."

64 A. Seldom have there been trades involving two future Hall of Famers; one occurred in December of 1926, when this man and Jimmy Ring went from the Giants to the Cards for Rogers Hornsby. In St. Louis he became an integral part of the "Gashouse Gang," serving as their player-manager for 5 of his 11 seasons there.

B. Known as the "Fordham Flash," he won the NL MVP in 1931. He also appeared in eight World Series.

C. Over his 19 seasons, he finished in the top five for stolen bases 14 times.

65 A. Steady and productive, this AL West outfielder who retired after the 2010 season always seemed to be underappreciated.

On average, projected for playing 162 games a year, he was usually good for around 20 HR and close to 100 RBIs yearly.

B. He was around so long, he played for the Angels when they were called California, Anaheim, and then Los Angeles of Anaheim. Through 2019, he was still the franchise leader in many categories including hits, doubles, runs, ribbies, and total bases.

C. He won the All-Star Game Home Run Derby in 2003, and twice led the AL in doubles with a dazzling high of 56 in 2002.

66 A. This man is the last player to hit .400 in the NL. He managed that in 1930, the Year of the Rabbit Ball.

B. A Hall of Fame first baseman who played exclusively for the New York Giants, he also hit an astronomical .341 lifetime (1923–36), bettering .350 on four occasions.

C. His big league career didn't really get into full swing until he was 26 years old, but he soon starred on both defense and offense. He was also a player-manager, and continued to manage after his playing days had ended.

67 A. In 1962, this outfielder had 106 RBIs by the second All-Star break (that year was one of the seasons in which there were two All-Star contests). That gave him a swelteringly hot average of exactly one run driven in per game his Dodgers had played up to that point.

B. This was also his first season with more than 460 at bats, and he ended the 1962 season with 153 RBIs, which was the most in NL play in 25 years. After that year, however, he never again touched the 90-RBI level.

C. He won batting titles in 1962 and 1963.

68 A. The day before the 1998 All-Star break, this power hitter topped the century mark for RBI (with 101) in his club's 87th game, when he homered twice off Randy Johnson. He ended the year with 157 RBIs.

B. That season was his fifth and final year, with 40+ homers. It was also the year he won his second AL MVP.

C. In the 1996 ALDS, he pummeled Yankee pitchers (.438, 5 HR, 9 RBIs), but New York prevailed over Texas.

69 A. This hard-throwing reliever was the first man to represent four teams in All-Star play, and he did so for teams from different divisions: the White Sox, Pirates, Yankees, and Padres.

B. A Hall of Famer, he finished with 310 saves and 115 wins in relief, then trailing only Hoyt Wilhelm and Lindy McDaniel.

C. In 1979, he and a Yankees teammate, the equally nails-tough Cliff Johnson, got into a widely publicized heavyweight bout in their clubhouse. Highly durable, he was still laboring in 1994 at the age of 42 with the M's.

70 A. He pitched for Seattle from 1999, breaking in at the age of 20, through 2006, winning 55 times.

B. He once went exactly one year between losses on the road. In 2003, he became the first pitcher since Whitey Ford (1953) to win 15 contests after missing the previous two seasons.

C. The Royals signed him to a five-year, $55 million contract beginning in 2007. His jersey number that season was 55, very symbolic considering his new deal. Skeptics, cynics, and critics noted that it was as if he was being rewarded to the tune of $1 million for each of his career 55 victories up to that point. Over his next two seasons for K.C., he won 23 and dropped 24. If you get this one, consider yourself a real pro.

71 A. No player has appeared in more no-hitters, 11, than this short-stop, who is mainly remembered for his days with the A's.

B. On September 8, 1965, he became the first player ever to play all nine positions during a single game. One report has him pitching with both arms in that contest.

C. In 1968, he led the AL in hits, albeit with only 177. Six times he led his league in steals. Finally, he gained notoriety during Game 2 of the 1972 ALCS when he threw his bat at pitcher Lerrin LaGrow after being drilled in the ankle by a pitch. He was suspended for the rest of that series and for the first seven games of the 1973 season, but was permitted to play in the '72 World Series. His A's won, but he hit a paltry .179.

72. A. In 2006, he grounded into a double play once every 239 plate appearances.

   B. In 2005, he broke out of the gate as if a starter pistol's blast had jolted him off the blocks. Rookie of the Year honors seemed inevitable when he was named April's Rookie of the Month, hitting .410.

   C. In early June of 2005, however, he was injured when he fell down the steps in his apartment building and broke his collarbone. He was out of action until September. His initials are C.B.

73. A. He is the only Hall of Famer with the initials "E.L.," and he has the same last name as a legendary NFL head coach.

   B. Notorious for being slow afoot, he still managed to twice lead the NL in hitting. He was the NL MVP in 1938 as well.

   C. A lifetime .306 hitter, he was also well known for his prominent nose, which was responsible for his nickname of "Schnozz."

74. A. Eddie Collins, Eric Young, Carl Crawford, and this man are the only ones to pilfer six bases in a single contest.

   B. He managed that feat on June 16, 1991, as a member of the Braves, but he played the outfield for a slew of other teams, never for long.

   C. Although he stole 620 bases (1983–99), he never once led his league in that department. Final clue: He shares his last name with an American president.

75. A. Reportedly, only three men, Denis Menke (who played every infield position), Pete Rose (first, second, third, and outfield), and this man were regulars at four different defensive positions. In this man's case, he played first, second, third, and the outfield.

B. He lasted from 1987 through 2000, broke in with the Mets, ended his career with the Tigers, and made the All-Star squad twice.

C. When he came onto the big league scene, much was made about his extensive and unusual training program that he underwent with his father's guidance. He would, for example, take swings as a lefty and a righty while standing in a swimming pool. They even simulated taking grounders off an artificial surface. "My dad would tape up balls with black electrician tape and it would kind of skip like you were on turf," he said.

$$\circ\circ\circ \ \mathbf{4} \ \circ\circ\circ$$

ANSWERS

1. Joe Charboneau

2. Eddie Stanky

3. Wally Backman

4. Mike Hampton. His megadeal, by the standards of his day, with Colorado called for $121 million over eight seasons.

5. Zane Smith, who, despite a decent career ERA of 3.74 and pretty good ratios of innings pitched to both strikeouts and hits surrendered, lost 115 games compared to his 100 victories.

6. "Smoky Joe" Wood. This star of the early days of the game was on pace for a Hall of Fame career until injury struck him.

7. Jim "Mudcat" Grant. He was making an issue of facial hair just as Bill Russell had "introduced the beard to the NBA," according to Richman.

8. Rex Hudler

9. Sterling Hitchcock

10. Walt Dropo. Only he and Pinky Higgins ever managed 12 consecutive hits. Dropo's streak, which took place about six weeks after the Red Sox traded him to Detroit in a nine-player transaction, began with a brilliant 5-for-5 day on July 14, 1952. That was followed by a hitting binge during a twin bill the next day: He went 4-for-4 in the first game, then slashed three more hits in a row

during a 4-for-5 outburst in the nightcap before his skein was snapped. Incidentally, the next day he added two more hits, giving him 15 over four contests to tie the AL record.

11 Gus Bell. His son Buddy starred for 18 seasons, retired in 1989, and has coached and/or managed and worked in the front office often since then.

12 Bob Boone. He is the son of Ray, an infielder (1948–60), and the father of Aaron and Bret, who played from 1992 through 2005 and amassed 1,021 RBIs, the most of any member of his family. The only other three-generation families to play at the major league level are the Hairstons: Jerry Hairston Jr. and his brother Scott are the sons of outfielder Jerry Hairston, and the grandsons of Sam Hairston, who played in the Negro American League before making it to the bigs briefly in 1951 as a catcher for the White Sox (their first African-American player ever) and the Colemans: Joe, Joe Jr., and Casey. In addition, two of the Hairston uncles played pro ball, with one of them, John, spending a short time in the majors with the Cubs.

13 Jeff Samardzija of Notre Dame

14 David Newhan

15 Matt Morris

16 Orel Hershiser, who had also won the Little League World Series.

17 Bobby Wine

18 Garry Maddox

19 Tim Keefe

20 Ozzie Smith

21 Jim Kaat. He is one of four men to win 25+ and *not* win the Cy Young Award.

22 Vinny Castilla

23 Lew Burdette

24 Mickey Lolich. The Tigers ace was Denny McLain, who went 31–6 in 1968, but it was Lolich who defeated the Cardinals three times

in October of that year, giving up just five runs over his three complete games. Since Lolich, only Randy Johnson has won three games in a Series, but, unlike Lolich, Johnson had a relief win tossed into his mix. By the way, when Lolich homered in the '68 Series, he became the first man to crack a homer in the World Series but never hit one during the regular season.

25 Dick Groat. For years he and second baseman Bill Mazeroski formed one of the greatest double-play combos ever.

26 Albert Pujols

27 Joe Adcock

28 Shawn Green

29 Doug Mientkiewicz

30 Ugueth Urbina. More than five months after kidnappers made their demands, a raid, which was carried out by 30 police officers, left one kidnapper dead and rescued Urbina's mother unharmed. As for his attempted murder charges, he was accused of participating in an attack (with a group of other men) on five workers at his family's ranch; the attackers allegedly injured the workers using machetes and poured gasoline on them as well. In March of 2007 he was sentenced to 14 years in prison.

31 Ron Hunt. From 1968 through 1974, his final season, he led the NL in getting hit by pitches every single year.

32 Coco Laboy. In the Expos' inaugural season, fans loved hearing his name and that of Boccabella over the PA. The announcer, for example, would stretch out the pronunciation of Boccabella so it sounded like "BOCK—A—BELLLL—AH." Such diversion had to pass for entertainment for the Expos faithful, as Montreal went 52–110, finishing in the basement of the NL East. In case you were wondering, Boston's Coco Crisp's real first name is Covelli.

33 Larvell Blanks

34 David Clyde. In high school he went 18–0 and gave up only three earned runs over 148 innings pitched.

35 Doug DeCinces

36 Mike Bordick. In 2002, when he was nearly flawless in the field—one error and a glowing .998 fielding percentage—he lost the Gold Glove to Alex Rodriguez, who committed 10 errors to go with his .987 fielding percentage.

37 Gene Tenace

38 Travis Hafner. He now stands as number one for the most homers hit by a player born in North Dakota (213), ahead of Darin Erstad. Despite a common misconception, Roger Maris, who hit 275 HR, lived in that state, but was not *born* there.

39 Mark Teixeira

40 Thurman Munson

41 Vernon Law. Trivia: He was the first pitcher to win an All-Star Game, World Series contest, and the Cy Young Award in the same season.

42 Nap Lajoie. On May 23, 1901, the White Sox, leading Lajoie's Athletics 11–7, walked Lajoie, who would hit over .400 that season, with the bases loaded and nobody out—a first. The unorthodox move worked when the next three batters were retired. The Cleveland team was known as the Naps from 1903 through 1914, and he was their player-manager from 1905 through 1909.

43 Todd Walker

44 Jim Thorpe. A trivia note about Toney: In 1909 he fired an incredible 19-inning no-hitter in the minors.

45 Joe Nuxhall. Although he was shelled in his first outing and was then shipped to the minors, he went on to return to the majors, but not until 1952. He then proceeded to put up some good numbers over his career (135 wins over 16 seasons). Meanwhile, the American League's youngest player was Carl Scheib, a 16-year-old who pitched sparingly for the A's in his rookie year, 1943.

46 Moose Skowron—he got his nickname because as a young boy he once got a haircut, which made him resemble Italian dictator Mussolini, and that name got shortened to Moose.

47 Bob Moose

48 Kerry Wood. His big game alluded to in the question was, of course, his record-tying 20-strikeout performance on May 6, 1998.

49 Vince Coleman. Only four men have stolen 100+ bases, and that feat has been done a total of seven times. Coleman did it three times, and did so in his first three seasons in the majors.

50 Bill White

51 Alex Johnson

52 Dick Stuart

53 Carlos Beltran

54 Tom Grieve. Incidentally, Grieve's trade of Sosa was endorsed by the Rangers' then co-managing general partner, George W. Bush.

55 Andy Messersmith

56 Burleigh Grimes

57 Wilbur Wood. No pitcher ever had more than his 18 wins (in 1973) at the All-Star break, yet he was not on the squad. He went on to win and lose 20 games that year, finishing at 24–20.

58 Luis Gonzalez

59 Chris Shelton

60 Elroy Face

61 Rick Wise

62 Chuck Klein

63 Al Simmons

64 Frankie Frisch. As a side note, Ring was also once traded along with a future Pro Football Hall of Famer, Earle "Greasy" Neale, then an outfielder, for yet another future Hall of Famer, pitcher Eppa Rixey.

65 Garret Anderson

66 Bill Terry

67 Tommy Davis. In high school he was a basketball star and teammate of future basketball Hall of Famer Lenny Wilkens.

68 Juan Gonzalez

69 Goose Gossage
70 Gil Meche
71 Bert Campaneris
72 Clint Barmes
73 Ernie Lombardi
74 Otis Nixon
75 Gregg Jefferies

⚾ ⚾ ⚾ **5** ⚾ ⚾ ⚾

EXTRA INNINGS

In this very brief chapter which is made up of 27 questions to correspond with the number of outs a team gets in a game, you're given one clue, one final pitch, and you either connect to crank a game-winning home run, or you whiff and all hope for victory dies out.

1 His real name was Harold, but this Hall of Famer third baseman went by a dessert-inspired nickname.

2 To continue the culinary theme, this slugging outfielder, whose son played basketball for the University of Maryland, shares his last name with that of a fruit.

3 Active from 1986 through 2012, this "ageless" (he retired at the age of 49), crafty southpaw is married to the daughter of former Notre Dame basketball coach Digger Phelps.

4 This A's reliever won the MVP and the Cy Young Award in the same season, 1992. Earlier in his career when he was a starter, he threw a no-hitter.

5 Mainly a third baseman for the Orioles who was an All-Star in 2003 and 2005, this man is the father of quintuplets. His initials are the same as the Yankee great who wore jersey number 7. Name him.

6 Through 2006, he was one of six active players with 10+ years in the majors who never spent a day on the disabled list—amazing since he's a catcher. He has three NL Gold Gloves and was an All-Star in Detroit. He later managed the Tigers and the Angels.

7 Even carrying 235 pounds on his 6' 3" frame, this graceful first baseman (1985–2004) deserved the nickname "Big Cat."

8 This man is a basketball Hall of Famer, but also pitched for the White Sox. His initials are D.D.

9 In 2006, these two brothers hit one-two in the Padres lineup on occasion. The older brother began his career with the Indians and was later with the Pirates. His first name starts with the letter "B." Can you identify either one or both of these brothers?

10 This southpaw retired in 2007, and through 2019 he is ranked No. 2 for all-time appearances, having taken to the mound in 1,178 games. His initials are M.S. Final clue: he spent seven seasons with both the Yankees and Braves.

11 Also early in 2007, this catcher moved into the number four slot for lifetime games caught.

12 This Hall of Famer, whose nickname was an article of clothing worn by players, is credited with the idea of having spring training. He was the first man to reach 3,000 hits.

13 In the 1960 World Series against the Pirates, a New York Yankee set records by driving in six runs in a single game and 12 overall, a figure which was nearly half as many as he had driven in all year (26). In an unprecedented move, he was named the MVP despite playing for the losing club.

14 He was the first man to hit 40+ HR in a season in the NL, with Atlanta, *and* in the AL, with Detroit. Initials: D.E.

15 This former Brave is the only pitcher ever to hit two grand slams in a game.

16 The brother of the only man to win batting titles in three decades (doing so in 1976, 1980, and 1990) is also the owner of

the record for the most consecutive games hitting a home run as a pitcher: four.

17 In 2004, this Astros righty set an NL record for the most Ks by a reliever, 157 in only 94 ⅔ innings. Many people speculated that after serving up a famous homer to Albert Pujols in the 2005 NLCS, the relief pitcher found it difficult to shake that off. He did rack up 32 saves the next season, but his ERA ballooned from 2.29 to 5.28.

18 In 1975, this Astros first baseman scored the one-millionth run in major league history.

19 In 1992 and '93, this Indians star joined Rogers Hornsby as the only second basemen to hit .300 with 20+ homers, 100+ RBIs, and 200+ hits in a season.

20 He was the oldest rookie ever, listed as being 42 when he made his debut in 1948, even though records of his exact date of birth were in question (e.g. one source has him as a 41-year-old rookie, but many felt he was much older).

21 In 2007, his first homer of the season made him, at the age of 48 years, eight months, and 12 days, the oldest player to hit a home run. He was already the oldest ever to belt a grand slam, doing that for the Braves in 2005.

22 On September 29, 1986, a first took place when two rookie starting pitchers who were brothers squared off against each other. The winner was Greg Maddux. The man in question is his older brother. Name him.

23 A mainstay as an announcer for the Giants, this former infielder owns the lowest lifetime home run percentage in the modern era, .00029—who is he?

24 In 1990, this speedy outfielder won a batting crown in one league, the NL, even though he finished the year in the AL after having put up enough plate appearances to qualify for his title.

25 In 1964, he became the first modern-day rookie to win a batting title. He hit .323 for the 1964 Twins.

26 This man, at the Methuselah-like age of 53, is the oldest to collect a hit in big league play. In a 1976 gimmick, he donned the White Sox uniform, was penciled in as their designated hitter, and managed one hit, a single, in eight at-bats.

27 There was a time in the 1960s that the Dodgers featured an infield made up entirely of switch-hitters. Jim Lefebvre was at third, Maury Wills was the shortstop, and Jim Gilliam handled the chores at second base. Name the first baseman.

$\circ \circ \circ$ **5** $\circ \circ \circ$

ANSWERS

1. Pie Traynor
2. Darryl Strawberry
3. Jamie Moyer. He endured 25 big league seasons and won 269 games.
4. Dennis Eckersley
5. Melvin Mora
6. Brad Ausmus
7. Andres Galarraga. This man was an All-Star five times, won two Gold Gloves, two Silver Slugger awards, and he tossed in a batting title as well when he punished the ball in 1993, hitting .370.
8. Dave DeBusschere
9. The brothers are Marcus and Brian Giles
10. Mike Stanton, a man who made just one big league start over his 19 seasons in the majors.
11. Ivan Rodriguez
12. Adrian "Cap" Anson
13. Bobby Richardson. Four of his RBIs came on a grand slam after he had fouled off a squeeze bunt.
14. Darrell Evans

15 Tony Cloninger. The day he hit his two grand slams to become the first NL player to accomplish this feat, he added a ninth run batted in during a 17–3 rout over the Giants. Those nine RBIs still represents a single game record for a pitcher. Through 2019, only 13 men have ever connected for two slams in a game. Only one player, Fernando Tatis, father of current player Fernando Tatis Jr., hit his two grand slams in the same inning.

16 Ken Brett, brother of Hall of Famer George Brett. He did it in June of 1973, and those were his only homers of the year.

17 Brad Lidge

18 Bob Watson

19 Carlos Baerga

20 Satchel Paige

21 Julio Franco

22 Mike Maddux

23 Duane Kuiper. His one homer over 3,379 at bats came at the expense of Cy Young winner Steve Stone.

24 Willie McGee

25 Tony Oliva

26 Minnie Minoso

27 Wes Parker

BONUS

Each one of the dozen questions in the bonus section pertains to players who were active in 2019 (with one exception—question 4). Be aware that none of the men discussed in this section appeared in the original edition of this book. The difficulty of the questions varies, so you have to be on your toes for each and every one. All statistics mentioned are through the 2019 season unless otherwise indicated.

1 A. This pitcher has been one of the most dominant ones in the NL since he broke into the majors in 2008 with a West Coast team. For example, he was an All-Star every season from 2011 through 2017, and again in 2019.

   B. He's even won four straight ERA crowns and he has posted ERAs below 2.00 three times. He also led his league in wins on three occasions.

   C. With Sandy Koufax-like numbers, it's no surprise this lefty has won three Cy Young Awards and, in 2011, won the Triple Crown of pitching, leading the league in wins, ERA, and strikeouts.

2 A. This outfielder "owns" numerous offensive categories. He started collecting hardware in 2012 as the Rookie of the Year. He has led the AL in a wide variety of categories including runs, steals, ribbies, walks drawn, slugging, and total bases. In 2019, he led his league in on-base percentage for the fourth year running and his lifetime OB% stands at a lofty .419. That season, he earned AL MVP accolades. Incidentally, he shares his last name with Steve and Dizzy.

B. In 2014, he was not only the MVP of the All-Star Game, he was also his league's MVP.

C. Here's the giveaway clue: in each of his first seven full seasons he's either won an MVP trophy or finished second, with the exception of an "off" year in 2017 when he came in fourth in the voting. By the way, that season he led his league in four major categories including on-base plus slugging at 1.071.

3 A. This man reached 100 lifetime homers faster than any Dodger in franchise history, doing so in his 401st game to break Mike Piazza's record of 422 contests.

B. In 2019 he had already hit his 40th home run by mid-August and had been named to his second All-Star Game over his first three seasons in the majors. He concluded the season with 47 HR and a league-leading 351 total bases.

C. This 2017 Rookie of the Year plays outfield and first base.

4 A. More than one expert has admitted that this slugger snuck up on them statistically speaking. That is to say, they were surprised when they began to realize he was closing in on major milestones such as reaching the 3,000-hit club, which he did in 2017.

B. He played for the Dodgers, Mariners (where he won two Gold Gloves for his outstanding play on the left side of the infield), Red Sox, and Rangers.

C. In 2004, when he led the NL in homers with 48 and established a personal high of 121 runs driven in, he finished second in MVP voting.

5 A. This man is one of three brothers who all played the same position. Like the player in question here, one of them was a Gold Glove recipient even though he won seven fewer of those awards than the subject of this question has done.

B. He's a solid hitter at .281 lifetime, but his ticket to the nine All-Star Games he's been selected to is his defense. As a matter of fact, he has won four Platinum Glove awards.

C. He also has come through with his bat in World Series play with a .328 batting average over 21 games, and in 2006 he helped his team dispose of the Tigers in five games, hitting .412.

6 A. Young and exciting, and with an infectious smile, this short-stop was a rookie in 2015. The very next year he earned a Platinum Glove and in 2019 he won his second Gold Glove.

B. He finished second in Rookie of the Year voting to a fellow shortstop. He's already been an AL All-Star four times, three times more than the man who did win the Rookie of the Year Award in 2015.

C. He is successful on around 80 percent of his stolen base attempts, but he has some clout, too. In 2018 he belted 38 homers while also topping the league in runs scored and coming in fourth in Wins Above Replacement. Despite being limited to 143 games in 2019, he still managed to hit 32 homers, giving him three straight 30+ HR seasons, not too shabby for a 5'11", 190 pound shortstop.

7 A. So good, so young, this man already has gone from being the Rookie of the Year in 2012 to winning an MVP Award just three years later.

B. In his MVP season, he led the NL in home runs (42), runs (118), on-base percentage (.460), slugging (1.109), and, of course, on-base plus slugging.

C. His colorful garb when he won a dramatic Home Run Derby in 2018 in front of a home crowd was the talk of baseball. However, 2019 found him in a uniform of a new team, the Phillies.

8 A. Baseball insiders rave about this infielder's incredible quick tags he applies to runners, most often taking place at second base.

B. He won a Silver Slugger Award in 2018 when he exploded for a league-leading 111 runs driven in, 36 more than he had for his previous high. His offensive stats slipped a bit in 2019, mainly due to his missing 24 games, but he was still an NL All-Star.

C. The Puerto Rico native is nicknamed "El Mago," which is Spanish for "The Magician."

9 A. This pitcher has played for the Tigers and Astros. In Detroit, he led the league in wins twice with an apex of 24 in 2011 when he lost only five times while also ranking number one for ERA, winning percentage (.828), strikeouts (250), WHIP (0.920), and innings pitched.

B. He was a first-round pick out of Old Dominion University who soon became a Rookie of the Year as well as a pitching Triple Crown winner and a Cy Young Award recipient. Toss in the fact that he has thrown three no-hitters (with the third one coming in 2019). In addition, the 2019 season featured him topping his league in wins with 21. Finally, he hit the rare 300 strikeout level in 2019, a total higher than what he achieved the four times he has led his league in that department.

C. OK, it had to been thrown in there: he gained off-the-field headlines by dating and marrying a famous model/actress.

10 A. Colorful and controversial, this outfielder with a howitzer for a right arm was involved in a big three-team trade in 2019 which also involved equally colorful and controversial pitcher Trevor Bauer. The swap marked the second time he was traded over a span of just seven months.

B. He's been known to kiss his bat and one time after giving it a smooch he jerked away from it, reacting to the horrible taste of pine tar. With his first big league club he would kiss his hitting coaches on the cheek or forehead upon returning to the dugout after homering. He even kissed a former teammate on his neck after being tagged out by a mile on a poorly executed delay steal of second!

C. His nickname is "Wild Horse."

11 A. He came to the majors by way of Stetson University, originally drafted by the Padres in 2007. Seven years later he won the first of his two Cy Young Awards.

B. In 2017, he won at a .818 clip based on 18 victories versus just four defeats, and he was first in the AL in ERA as well. That earned him his second Cy Young trophy.

C. Unemotional on the mound, the dependable right-hander who led the league in innings pitched in 2018 was thwarted and frustrated in 2019 when injuries kept him sidelined for a large chunk of the season.

12 A. The man in question who bats lefty but throws righty is normally stationed at first base, and he plays his position well as his 2018 Gold Glove Award attests. During that same year, he smashed 44 doubles to stand atop the NL, and he also had more hits, 191, than any other NL player. It helped that he played in all 162 games on the schedule that season (just as he had done in 2014).

B. He's been with the same organization since he was drafted by them in 2007. In his first season in the majors, his teammates included Brian McCann, Jason Heyward, Troy Glaus, Melky Cabrera, and Martin Prado.

C. Only 24 position players who were active in 2019 had a better WAR than this man whose first and last names start with the same letter.

ANSWERS

1. Clayton Kershaw. Many consider him to be the closest Dodger pitcher ever to Sandy Koufax as far as sheer ability and statistics go. In fact, by mid-August of 2019 both men had exactly 165 victories under their belts and Kershaw, nearing the end of his 12th season, actually had a higher winning percentage at .699 (he finished the year with a lifetime mark of .695) to .655 for Koufax, who lasted 12 years in the majors. Koufax posted a lifetime ERA of 2.76 versus Kershaw's 2.44 (through 2019), but Koufax had a slight edge in number of times leading the league in a significant statistical category.

2. Mike Trout

3. Cody Bellinger

4. Adrian Beltre. He ranked No. 13 lifetime in defensive WAR and he became just the fourth third baseman to hit 400 or more homers and drive in 1,500+ runs. Until fellow Dominican Albert Pujols passed him on the all-time hit list in 2019, Beltre owned the most lifetime hits by a player born outside the United States.

5. Yadier Molina

6. Francisco Lindor, a man so bubbly his nickname is "Mr. Smile."

7. Bryce Harper

8. Javier Baez

9 Justin Verlander. His model/actress wife is, of course, Kate Upton.

10 Yasiel Puig

11 Corey Kluber. He earned the nickname Klubot for the stoical and nearly robotic way he goes about his pitching duties. In the 2016 World Series he became the first pitcher to methodically mow down eight batters on strikes over the first three innings. The only out of the first nine which didn't come via a K was a harmless pop fly.

12 Freddie Freeman

ABOUT THE AUTHOR

Wayne Stewart was born and raised in Donora, Pennsylvania, a town that has produced several big league baseball players, including Stan Musial and the father-son Griffeys. Stewart now lives in Lorain, Ohio, and is married to Nancy (Panich) Stewart. They have two sons, Sean and Scott.

He has covered the sports world as a writer for more than 30 years, beginning in 1978. He has interviewed and profiled many stars, including Kareem Abdul-Jabbar and Larry Bird, as well as numerous baseball legends such as Nolan Ryan, Bob Gibson, Tony Gwynn, Greg Maddux, Rickey Henderson, and Ken Griffey Jr.

In addition, Stewart has written more than 20 baseball books and one book on basketball. Some of his works have also appeared in seven baseball anthologies, one which has sold over 70,000 copies to date. He has also written over 500 articles for publications such as *Baseball Digest, USA Today/Baseball Weekly, Boys' Life*, and Beckett Publications.

He has written for many major league official team publications, such as the Braves, Yankees, White Sox, Orioles, Padres, Twins, Phillies, Red Sox, A's, and Dodgers. Furthermore, Stewart has appeared as a baseball expert/historian on Cleveland's Fox 8, on an ESPN Classic television show on Bob Feller, and on numerous radio shows. He also hosted his own radio shows, including a call-in sports talk show, a pregame Indians report, and pregame shows for Notre Dame football. You can find him at https://waynestewartonsports.blog/.

NOTES

NOTES

NOTES

NOTES

NOTES